This Textbook is useful for Savitribai Phule Pune University and other Universities of Maharashtra as well as Competitive Exams.

History

Art and Architecture in Medieval India

(HIS - 558 MJ)

M.A. - I (Sem. - II)

As per New Education Policy (2020)

Prof. Prashant Pawar

(B.Sc., L.L.B., M.A. (AIH & C), M.A. (History), L.L.M.(Buss. Law), M.Phil., SET)

MVP Samaj's Arts, Commerce and Science College, Tryambakeshwar, Nashik.

2023

Price -115/-

SUCCESS PUBLICATIONS

Published by
Dr. Rajesh M. Patne
Success Publications
Radha Krishna Apartment, 535, Shaniwar Peth,
Appa Balwant Chowk, Opp. Prabhat Talkies, Pune - 411 030.
Ph. 24434662, Mobile : 9325315464.

Edition
2023

Edited By
Mr. Valmik Gaikwad

Typesetting, Layout
Miss. Sayali Bhosale

Cover Designing
Miss. Varsha Lokhande

ISBN NO. – 978-81-19939-00-8

Preface

It is a matter of great pleasure for us to present this book to our esteemed readers. This book has been designed as standard text on 'Art and Architecture in Medieval India' for M. A. (History) (Sem. - II).

This book comprehensively covers the entire syllabus of M.A. (History) Course of Savitribai Phule Pune University effective from 2023 onwards. It has been written to meet the requirements of students of M. A. (History). Some of the special features of the book are as follows:

1. *Full coverage of the revised syllabus of M. A. (History).*
2. *Chapter outline at the beginning of each chapter to give a bird's eye view of the topics covered in the chapter.*
3. *Point wise explanation of each topic in the chapter.*
4. *Topics are logically arranged in numbered paragraphs exactly according to the modified syllabus.*
5. *Proposed questions at the end of each chapter.*
6. *Extensive use of diagrams, tables and various forms to give visual view of key concepts and techniques.*
7. *Conversational, lucid and simple language.*

Every effort has been made to provide the readers with most up-to-date and authentic material on the subject.

We are very grateful to our publisher Mrs. and Mr. Rajesh Patne who have rendered all possible assistance in bringing out this book. We wish to acknowledge our deep gratitude to staff who have assisted and helped us in preparing this book. We will consider our efforts amply rewarded in case the book proves useful to the students and teachers of the subject.

Suggestions of readers are welcome and shall be acknowledged with gratitude.

With best wishes.

By Authors

Syllabus

M. A. - I (Sem. - II) History

Art and Architecture in Medieval India (HIS-558 MJ)

Unit	Topic	Lecture
1	**Introduction to Medieval Indian Art and Architecture**	10
	a. Technique of making Arches and domes b. Quwwat-ul-Islam Masjid c. Tomb of Iltumish d. Qutub Minar e. Alai Darwaza	
2	**Emergence and Development of Deccan Art & Architecture**	08
	a. Bahamani b. Vijaynagar c. Maratha	
3	**Development of Sur and Mughal Art & Architecture**	12
	a. Qila-i-Kuhna Masjid, Tombs of Hasan Sur and Sher Shah b. Akbar: The Tomb of Humayan, Agra Fort, Fatehpur Sikri, Allahabad and Lahore forts c. Jahangir: Sikandara, Tomb of Itmad-ud-Daula d. Shahjahan: The Taj Mahal, Red Fort, Jama Masjid e. Mughal Paintings f. Regional Art & Architecture	

INDEX

M. A. - I (Sem. - II) History
Art and Architecture in Medieval India (HIS-558 MJ)

UNIT 1
Introduction to Medieval Indian Art and Architecture

Introduction:

Medieval Indian art and architecture, spanning over a millennium from the 6th to the 16th century, is a mesmerizing tapestry of cultural, religious, and architectural influences. It reflects the diversity and rich heritage of the Indian subcontinent, characterized by a synthesis of indigenous traditions with external elements. During this period, several powerful dynasties and empires, such as the Gupta, Chola, Pallava, Rashtrakuta, Hoysala, and Mughal, left an indelible mark on the artistic landscape. Hindu, Buddhist, Jain, and Islamic faiths coexisted, leading to a remarkable blend of architectural styles and artistic expressions. Key features include intricate temple architecture with distinctive shikharas (towering spires), intricate carvings, and exquisite sculptures that capture divine narratives and mythological tales. Notable examples include the rock-cut temples at Ellora and Ajanta, the Sun Temple at Konark, and the exquisite Khajuraho temples. Islamic architecture also flourished during this era, marked by the grandeur of the Delhi Sultanate's Qutb Minar and the resplendent Mughal monuments like the Taj Mahal, which exemplify the fusion of Persian, Central Asian, and Indian architectural elements. Medieval Indian art and architecture bear witness to a vibrant, evolving, and enduring legacy that continues to captivate and inspire admirers around the world.

1.1 Techniques of Making Arches and Domes:

The construction of arches and domes involves intricate architectural techniques that have evolved over centuries. Arches, with their curved structures, rely on the precise placement of wedge-shaped stones or bricks, culminating in a keystone at the apex, which distributes weight evenly, creating stability and allowing for open spans. Domes, on the other hand, come in various shapes like hemispherical, spherical, or onion, and their construction methods encompass masonry, thin-shell concrete and innovative materials like glass and steel. Domes may employ pendentives or rely on a network of arches or ribs to transfer loads to the supporting structure. Modern technology and computational design tools have further expanded the possibilities in creating these architectural wonders, while sustainability and preservation efforts ensure the enduring legacy of these iconic architectural forms.

1.1.1 Techniques of Making Arches:

Constructing arches is an ancient architectural practice that has played a significant role in shaping the built environment throughout history. Arches are not only structurally important but also add aesthetic and artistic value to buildings. Arches are architectural elements characterized by their curved or semicircular shape, serving both functional and decorative purposes. They are integral components of numerous architectural styles and have been used across different civilizations throughout history. The primary function of arches is to distribute loads and provide structural stability, making them a fundamental aspect of architectural design.

A) Historical Evolution of Arches:

Following are the key points of historic evolution of arches:

1) Ancient Civilizations:

The use of arches dates back to ancient civilizations like Mesopotamia and Egypt, where they were employed in constructing aqueducts, bridges, and monumental structures. The Roman civilization, however, made significant advancements in arch construction, perfecting the technique and popularizing it throughout their vast empire.

2) Roman Arch Innovation:

The Romans are renowned for their mastery of arch construction. They introduced the concept of the keystone, which is a wedge-shaped stone at the apex of an arch. The keystone locks the other stones in place and ensures structural stability. The Roman Arch, with its semicircular shape and voussoirs (wedge-shaped stones), became a hallmark of Roman architecture.

3) Byzantine and Islamic Influence:

After the fall of the Roman Empire, the Byzantine Empire continued to employ arches in their architecture, often using them in conjunction with domes. Islamic architecture also adopted the use of arches, with the horseshoe arch being a distinctive feature.

4) Gothic Arch Innovation:

In the Gothic period, architecture in Europe saw the development of pointed arches, which allowed for taller and more intricate cathedrals. The structural innovation of ribbed vaults and flying buttresses further supported the use of pointed arches.

5) Renaissance and Beyond:

The Renaissance period witnessed a revival of classical architectural forms, including semicircular arches, while subsequent architectural styles continued to incorporate arches in various ways, from Baroque to Neoclassical to Modern architecture.

B) Architectural Principles of Arch Construction:

Following are the architectural principles of arch construction:

1) Keystone and Voussoirs:

The keystone is the central, wedge-shaped stone at the top of an arch. It is crucial for maintaining the stability of the arch. Voussoirs are the wedge-shaped stones that make up the arch, with each successive voussoir exerting pressure on the ones below, which ultimately transfers the load to the supporting abutments.

2) Abutments:

Arches require solid supports called abutments at their endpoints. These abutments are responsible for resisting the outward thrust generated by the arch and keeping it in place.

3) Types of Arches:

Several arch types exist, including the semicircular arch, pointed arch (Gothic arch), horseshoe arch (Moorish arch), and segmental arch, each with its unique aesthetic and structural characteristics.

C) Materials Used in Arch Construction:

Following material used in arch construction:

1) Stone:

Stone has been a traditional material for arch construction due to its durability and load-bearing capacity. Stones like limestone, granite, and sandstone are commonly used.

2) Brick:

Brick arches are prevalent in various architectural styles. Bricks offer versatility in design and can be laid in various patterns, such as the header stretcher bond or the Flemish bond.

3) Concrete:

Modern arch construction often utilizes concrete, which can be molded into various arch shapes. Reinforced concrete, incorporating steel reinforcement bars (rebar), provides additional strength.

4) **Wood:**

Timber arches are less common but have been used historically, particularly in bridges and certain types of roofs. Timber arches require careful design and maintenance to prevent decay.

5) **Steel:**

Steel arches offer a high degree of strength and flexibility in design. They are commonly used in contemporary and industrial settings, such as bridges and large-scale infrastructure.

D) **Construction Techniques for Arches:**

Medieval India employed various construction techniques for arches, showcasing architectural prowess. Some prevalent methods included:

1) **Corbelled Arches:**

This technique involved layering stones or bricks in a stepped, corbelled manner, gradually reducing the span until the two sides met at the top, forming an arch-like structure. It was commonly seen in forts, temples, and palaces.

2) **True Arch Construction:**

Skilled masons crafted true arches using wedge-shaped stones or bricks, forming a curved structure that distributed weight efficiently. These were prominent in mosques, tombs, and monumental structures, showcasing a higher level of architectural sophistication.

3) **Multifoil and Trefoil Arches:**

Intricately designed arches with multiple lobes or cusps, known as multifoil or trefoil arches, were prevalent in Islamic architecture. They displayed decorative elements while distributing weight effectively, seen in mosques and tombs.

4) **Horseshoe Arch:**

Featured predominantly in Indo-Islamic architecture, the horseshoe arch displayed a rounded top with slightly pointed edges, symbolizing a fusion of local and Islamic architectural styles.

5) **Brickwork and Keystone Techniques:**

Use of well-shaped bricks and precise placement, often with a central keystone, created sturdy and aesthetically pleasing arches. The keystone served as a crucial element in maintaining the arch's structural integrity.

6) **Vaulted Arches:**

Employed in larger constructions like halls and gateways, vaulted arches utilized a series of adjoining arches to form a continuous ceiling or roof, distributing weight evenly.

7) **Roman Arch Construction:**

The construction of a traditional Roman arch typically involves creating a wooden form, known as centering, that supports the stones or bricks during construction.

The voussoirs are placed one by one, with the keystone inserted last. As the keystone is positioned, the arch springs into place, and the centering can be removed.

8) **Gothic Arch Construction:**
Pointed or Gothic arches are constructed similarly to Roman arches but have a taller and more pointed profile. Gothic arches often appear in cathedral architecture, emphasizing height and verticality.

9) **Masonry and Masonry Bonding:**
Masonry arches rely on the precise arrangement of bricks or stones. Common masonry bonds for arches include the header stretcher bond, the Flemish bond, and the English bond, each offering different aesthetic patterns and structural stability.

10) **Reinforced Concrete Arch Construction:**
Modern arches often employ reinforced concrete, which combines steel reinforcement (rebar) with concrete to create robust and versatile arch structures. The concrete is molded into the desired arch shape and allowed to cure, providing the necessary compressive strength.

E) **Notable Types of Arches:**
Following are the types of arches:

1) **Semicircular Arch:**
The semicircular arch has a classic rounded shape and is commonly found in Roman and Neoclassical architecture. It provides excellent structural stability.

2) **Pointed Arch (Gothic Arch):**
The pointed arch has a distinct pointed top and is associated with Gothic architecture. It allows for greater height and flexibility in architectural design.

3) **Horseshoe Arch (Moorish Arch):**
The horseshoe arch is characterized by its rounded shape with an extended base. It is a prominent feature in Islamic architecture, particularly in Spain and North Africa.

4) **Segmental Arch:**
The segmental arch has a shallow curve and is often used in openings like doors and windows. It is popular in both classical and modern architecture.

F) **Challenges and Innovations in Arch Construction:**
Following are the challenges of arch construction:

1) **Structural Challenges:**
Arch construction requires precise engineering to ensure stability and durability. The structural integrity of an arch depends on factors such as material selection, load distribution, and environmental conditions.

2) **Innovations in Materials:**
Modern arch construction benefits from advanced materials, including reinforced concrete and steel, allowing for greater architectural freedom and structural efficiency.

3) **Digital Design and Analysis:**

Contemporary architects and engineers use digital tools and software for the design and analysis of arches, ensuring optimal structural performance and aesthetics.

4) **Sustainable Practices:**

Sustainable building practices are becoming increasingly important in arch construction, with a focus on environmentally friendly materials and energy-efficient design.

5) **Artistic Expression:**

Arches continue to serve as vehicles for artistic expression, with architects and designers exploring innovative and unconventional arch forms in contemporary architecture.

1.1.2 Techniques of Making Domes:

Constructing domes is a fascinating and intricate aspect of architectural design and engineering that has captivated architects, builders, and civilizations throughout history. Domes are architectural marvels, known for their elegance, strength, and ability to span large spaces without the need for internal supports. Domes are architectural elements characterized by their curved, often spherical or hemispherical shape. They are employed both for structural stability and aesthetic appeal, offering a unique blend of beauty and functionality. Domes have been used across cultures and time periods, making them a testament to human ingenuity and architectural innovation.

A) **Historical Evolution of Domes:**

Following are the key points of historical evolution of domes:

1) **Ancient Origins:**

The use of domes can be traced back to ancient civilizations, with examples found in Mesopotamia and the Mediterranean region. The ancient Romans, in particular, developed advanced techniques for constructing domes, as evidenced by the Pantheon in Rome.

2) **Byzantine Domes:**

The Byzantine Empire embraced the use of domes in religious architecture, notably in the construction of churches like Hagia Sophia in Constantinople (modern-day Istanbul). Byzantine domes featured innovative structural elements like pendentives, which facilitated the transition from square or polygonal bases to circular domes.

3) **Islamic Influence:**

Islamic architecture adopted and adapted dome construction techniques from earlier civilizations. Notable examples include the Dome of the Rock in Jerusalem and the various domes found in mosques and palaces across the Islamic world.

4) **Renaissance and Baroque Periods:**

The Renaissance period saw a revival of classical architectural forms, including the use of domes. Architectural pioneers like Filippo Brunelleschi demonstrated remarkable engineering skills in constructing the dome of Florence Cathedral. The Baroque era added ornate embellishments to domes, as seen in St. Peter's Basilica in Rome.

5) **Modern Innovations:**

In the modern era, architects and engineers have continued to explore innovative dome structures. Geodesic domes, popularized by Buckminster Fuller, use a network of triangles to create lightweight and efficient structures. Contemporary architects have pushed the boundaries of dome design using advanced materials and computational design tools.

B) **Architectural Principles of Dome Construction:**

Following are the architectural principles of domes construction:

1) **Geometric Shape:**

Domes are typically hemispherical or spherical in shape. The choice of geometry affects the structural integrity and aesthetics of the dome.

2) **Supporting Structure:**

The supporting structure for a dome can vary. It may consist of solid walls, columns, or a system of arches and pendentives that transfer the load of the dome to the supporting structure below.

3) **Materials:**

Domes can be constructed using a variety of materials, including stone, brick, concrete, glass, and steel. The choice of material depends on factors such as structural requirements, architectural aesthetics, and available resources.

C) **Types of Domes:**

Following are the types of domes:

1) **Hemispherical Domes:**

Hemispherical domes have a half-sphere shape and are commonly found in classical and historic architecture. They offer structural stability and even distribution of loads.

2) **Spherical Domes:**

Spherical domes are complete spheres and are relatively rare due to their engineering complexity. The geodesic dome, designed by Buckminster Fuller, is a notable example of a spherical dome.

3) **Onion Domes:**

Onion domes are bulbous and pointed domes often associated with Russian and Eastern European architecture. They are typically constructed using a series of curved, stacked rings.

4) Ribbed Domes:

Ribbed domes feature a network of ribs or arches that create a skeletal structure supporting the dome's exterior shell. This design allows for intricate patterns and decorative elements.

5) Thin-Shell Domes:

Thin-shell domes are characterized by their lightweight, curved surfaces. They are often constructed using reinforced concrete or other modern materials and are known for their efficiency in spanning large spaces.

D) Materials Used in Dome Construction:

Following are the material used in dome construction:

1) Stone:

Stone domes, such as those found in ancient and medieval architecture, rely on carefully cut and stacked stones to create a self-supporting structure. The weight of the stones and their interlocking design provide stability.

2) Brick:

Brick domes are constructed by laying bricks in a curved pattern. The interlocking bricks distribute loads evenly and can create decorative patterns.

3) Concrete:

Modern dome construction frequently employs concrete, which can be molded into various dome shapes. Reinforced concrete, with embedded steel reinforcement bars (rebar), is commonly used for its strength and flexibility.

4) Glass and Steel:

Some contemporary designs incorporate glass and steel to create transparent or semi-transparent domes. These materials allow for natural light to filter into the interior space.

E) Construction Techniques for Domes:

In medieval India, constructing domes involved advanced architectural techniques and craftsmanship. Some prevalent methods used for dome construction included:

1) Circumferential Hooping:

Builders used wooden or iron rings, known as circumferential hooping, to support the base of the dome during construction. These rings, placed at different levels, provided temporary support until the dome was completed.

2) Persian/Double Dome Technique:

This method involved constructing an inner and outer dome, providing structural stability and insulation. The space between the two domes often served as a passageway or facilitated ventilation, seen in structures like the Gol Gumbaz in Bijapur.

3) **Drum Construction:**
Domes were often built on a raised, cylindrical base called a drum. The drum served as a transition from the square or rectangular base of the building to the curved shape of the dome, providing stability and support.

4) **Use of Squinches and Pendentives:**
Builders employed squinches (arched or angular supports at the corners of a square structure) or pendentives (curved triangles transitioning from a square base to a circular dome) to facilitate the transition from a square base to a circular dome, creating a seamless structural connection.

5) **Brickwork and Keystone Techniques:**
Skilled masons meticulously arranged and interlocked bricks in a circular or polygonal pattern, gradually forming the dome. The placement of a central keystone often held the structure together, providing stability and support.

6) **Finial and Decorative Elements:**
Elaborate finials, often in the form of decorative spires or ornaments, were placed atop domes for both aesthetic and functional purposes, adding to the grandeur and elegance of the structures while sometimes serving as lightning rods.

7) **Masonry Dome Construction:**
Masonry domes are built by layering stones or bricks in a radial pattern. The stones or bricks are progressively smaller as they approach the top of the dome. Gravity and the shape of the dome distribute the weight evenly, making it stable.

8) **Pendentive Dome Construction:**
Pendentives are triangular sections that facilitate the transition from a square or polygonal base to a circular dome. Pendentive domes are common in Byzantine and Islamic architecture, where they transfer the dome's load to the supporting walls or columns.

9) **Thin-Shell Concrete Dome Construction:**
Modern thin-shell concrete domes are often constructed using a formwork or mold that defines the desired dome shape. Concrete is poured into the mold and allowed to cure, resulting in a lightweight yet strong structure.

10) **Geodesic Dome Construction:**
Geodesic domes are assembled using a network of triangles, often made from steel or other lightweight materials. The triangular elements distribute loads efficiently and allow for a wide range of sizes and configurations.

F) **Challenges and Innovations in Dome Construction:**
Following are the challenges of domes construction:

1) **Structural Challenges:**
Dome construction requires precise engineering to ensure stability and durability. Factors such as material selection, load distribution, and seismic considerations must be carefully evaluated.

2) Geometric Complexity:

Designing complex dome shapes, especially non-spherical or non-hemispherical forms, can be challenging. Advanced computational design tools and digital modeling have facilitated the exploration of intricate geometries.

3) Sustainability and Energy Efficiency:

Sustainable building practices have become increasingly important in dome construction. Strategies include using environmentally friendly materials, optimizing natural lighting, and incorporating energy-efficient HVAC systems.

4) Restoration and Preservation:

Preserving historic domes presents unique challenges. Restoration efforts often require a deep understanding of the original construction techniques and materials used.

5) Innovations in Materials and Fabrication:

Advances in materials science and fabrication technologies have expanded the possibilities for dome construction. New materials, such as carbon fiber composites, offer enhanced strength and reduced weight.

6) Integration of Technology:

Architects and engineers are increasingly using digital tools for dome design, analysis, and construction planning. Computer-aided design (CAD) software, finite element analysis (FEA), and Building Information Modeling (BIM) play crucial roles in dome construction today.

1.2 Quwwat-ul-Islam Masjid:

Quwwat-ul-Islam Masjid, also known as the Qutub Mosque, is a historic mosque located in Delhi, India. This architectural marvel holds a special place in India's rich cultural and historical heritage. Following are the key points of Quwwat-ul Islam Masjid:

A) Historical Context:

The story of Quwwat-ul-Islam Masjid begins in the 12th century when Delhi was under the rule of Qutb-ud-din Aibak. Aibak was a prominent military general who served under Muhammad Ghori, the founder of the Ghurid Empire in India. Following Ghori's demise, Aibak established the Delhi Sultanate in 1192 and became its first Sultan.

1) The Construction of Quwwat-ul-Islam Masjid:

One of Aibak's significant contributions was the construction of Quwwat-ul-Islam Masjid, which translates to "The Might of Islam Mosque." This mosque was erected in close proximity to the Qutb Minar complex, a UNESCO World Heritage site that houses a plethora of historical structures.

2) Unique Architectural Fusion:

The architectural style of Quwwat-ul-Islam Masjid is strikingly unique, as it represents a fusion of Indian and Islamic elements. The most intriguing aspect is the incorporation of materials from demolished Hindu and Jain temples into the mosque's construction.

3) The Main Prayer Hall:

At the heart of Quwwat-ul-Islam Masjid lies a spacious open courtyard that surrounds the main prayer hall. The prayer hall itself is a testament to architectural mastery, adorned with intricately carved pillars and arches. These pillars, in particular, are repurposed from the ruins of Hindu and Jain temples, giving them a distinct appearance.

4) The Mihrab and Mehrab Screen:

Another remarkable feature of the mosque is the mihrab, an ornate niche in the mosque's wall that indicates the direction of Mecca. The mihrab is adorned with intricate calligraphy and geometric designs, showcasing the artistic prowess of the time. In front of the mihrab stands the mehrab screen, a finely carved stone screen that serves as a divider between the mihrab and the rest of the prayer hall.

5) The Qutb Minar Complex:

Quwwat-ul-Islam Masjid is an integral part of the larger Qutb Minar complex, which comprises several historically significant structures. The most iconic among them is the Qutb Minar itself, a towering minaret that stands as a symbol of Islamic architecture. The complex also houses the Iron Pillar of Delhi, renowned for its corrosion resistance and inscriptions, and various other historical edifices.

B) Significance and Cultural Importance:

Following are the significance & cultural importance of Quwwat-ul masjid:

1) A Symbol of Islamic Dominance:

Quwwat-ul-Islam Masjid served as a potent symbol of Islamic dominance and the establishment of the Delhi Sultanate in India. Its construction using materials salvaged from Hindu and Jain temples was a deliberate assertion of the supremacy of Islam over indigenous religions.

2) Preservation of Heritage:

Paradoxically, while Quwwat-ul-Islam Masjid represents Islamic dominance, it also played a role in preserving the architectural and artistic heritage of the region. The assimilation of elements from Hindu and Jain temples into Islamic architecture reflects the harmonious coexistence and interaction of diverse cultural influences in medieval India.

3) UNESCO World Heritage Site:

In recognition of its historical and architectural significance, Quwwat-ul-Islam Masjid is designated as a UNESCO World Heritage site. This prestigious designation underscores its importance as a cultural and historical treasure that must be preserved for future generations.

4) **Architectural Legacy:**
The mosque, built in the 12th century by Qutub-ud-din Aibak, was one of the earliest mosques constructed in India during the Delhi Sultanate era. It stands as a testament to early Indo-Islamic architecture, displaying a blend of Indian and Islamic architectural styles, evident in its distinctive arches, pillars, and domes.

5) **Adaptive Reuse of Materials:**
A significant aspect of Quwwat-ul-Islam Mosque's historical significance lies in its construction using materials from demolished Hindu and Jain temples, showcasing the adaptive reuse of architectural elements. The mosque's pillars, adorned with intricate carvings, were originally part of these temples, illustrating the assimilation of diverse cultural influences.

6) **Technological Advancements:**
The architectural techniques employed in constructing the mosque, particularly the innovative use of iron in the construction of its iconic Iron Pillar, which has stood rust-free for centuries, attests to the technological advancements of the time and continues to fascinate scientists and historians.

7) **Cultural Symbolism:**
Beyond its architectural significance, the mosque embodies cultural symbolism, reflecting India's rich heritage, architectural diversity, and the interplay between different civilizations and traditions that have shaped the country's cultural landscape over centuries.

C) **Cultural and Religious Impact:**
Following are the key points of cultural and religious impact of Quwwat-ul-islam masjid:

1) **Continued Religious Practices**
Quwwat-ul-Islam Masjid remains a place of active worship for Muslims in Delhi. The expansive prayer hall can accommodate a significant number of worshippers during Friday prayers and other religious gatherings. The serene ambiance and historical aura of the mosque make it a spiritually significant place for the local Muslim community.

2) **A Popular Tourist Attraction**
The mosque also draws tourists from around the world, eager to explore India's rich cultural heritage. Visitors are captivated by the intricate architectural details and the historical significance of the site. Quwwat-ul-Islam Masjid, along with the Qutb Minar complex, is an essential stop on Delhi's tourism circuit.

D) **Restoration and Conservation Efforts:**
Following are the key points of restoration and conservation efforts:

1) **Challenges of Preservation**
Over the centuries, Quwwat-ul-Islam Masjid has faced numerous challenges related to conservation and preservation. Weathering, pollution, and the ravages of time

have taken their toll on the mosque's architectural elements. Additionally, the heavy influx of tourists poses a risk to the structural integrity of the site.

2) **Conservation Initiatives**

To address these challenges, various governmental and non-governmental organizations have initiated comprehensive conservation efforts. These initiatives encompass cleaning, restoration of damaged carvings, and measures to control visitor access. The overarching goal is to ensure the long-term preservation of this historical gem.

1.3 Tomb of Iltumis:

The Tomb of Iltutmish, located in Delhi, India, is a historically significant architectural masterpiece that represents the early Indo-Islamic architectural style. Constructed primarily of red sandstone, its square layout is enclosed within an octagonal courtyard adorned with arched openings symbolizing the eight paradises of Islam. The central dome, crowned with an inverted lotus finial, is the focal point of the tomb and showcases intricate plasterwork on its interior. The structure bears Persian inscriptions, including an epitaph honoring Shams-ud-din Iltutmish, the third ruler of the Delhi Sultanate, and Quranic verses that underline its religious significance. As a UNESCO World Heritage Site, it holds profound historical and cultural importance, offering a glimpse into the architectural evolution and the enduring legacy of Iltutmish in the early years of Muslim rule in northern India.

1.3.1 Features of Tomb of Iltumis:

The Tomb of Itimad-ud-Daulah, often referred to as the "Baby Taj," is a historic mausoleum located in Agra, India. It is a stunning example of Mughal architecture and is known for its intricate design and exquisite craftsmanship. Here are key features of the Tomb of Itimad-ud-Daulah:

1) **Architectural Style:**

The Tomb of Itimad-ud-Daulah is a prime example of Mughal architecture, characterized by its use of white marble, intricate carvings, and symmetrical design. It represents a transition between the earlier Mughal architecture and the more famous Taj Mahal, which was built later.

2) **White Marble Construction:**

The tomb is constructed primarily from white marble, which gives it a pristine and ethereal appearance. This use of marble is a hallmark of Mughal architecture and adds to the tomb's aesthetic appeal.

3) **Garden Setting:**

The tomb is set within a Charbagh (four-quartered) garden, a classic Mughal garden layout. The garden is divided into four quadrants by water channels and pathways, creating a sense of harmony and symmetry.

4) **Water Features:**

Water plays a significant role in the garden's design. The garden features reflecting pools, water channels, and fountains, which not only enhance the visual appeal but also serve as a cooling element during hot weather.

5) **Intricate Inlay Work:**

The interior and exterior of the tomb are adorned with intricate inlay work, featuring delicate patterns and designs made from semi-precious stones like lapis lazuli and mother-of-pearl. This craftsmanship reflects the artistic excellence of the Mughal era.

6) **Hexagonal Towers:**

The tomb is flanked by hexagonal towers at each corner, adding an interesting architectural element to the structure. These towers are topped with elegant chhatris (domed pavilions) that enhance the overall beauty of the tomb.

7) **Jali (Lattice Work):**

The tomb's windows and screens feature finely carved jali (lattice work) that allows light to filter through while providing privacy to the interior spaces. This jali work is a testament to the Mughals' mastery of stone carving.

8) **Floral Motifs:**

The tomb is adorned with intricate floral motifs and designs, including vines, leaves, and flowers. These motifs are a common feature in Mughal architecture and add a sense of natural beauty to the structure.

9) **Historical Significance:**

The Tomb of Itimad-ud-Daulah is historically significant as it is the burial place of Mirza Ghiyas Beg, a Persian noble who served as the chief minister (Itimad-ud-Daulah) in the Mughal court during the reign of Emperor Jahangir. It is also the resting place of his wife Asmat Begum.

10) **Influence on the Taj Mahal:**

Many consider the Tomb of Itimad-ud-Daulah as a precursor and source of inspiration for the more famous Taj Mahal, which was built later by Emperor Shah Jahan in memory of his wife Mumtaz Mahal. The similarities in architectural elements and design between the two monuments are evident.

1.3.2 Historical Significance of Tomb of Iltumis:

The Tomb of Itimad-ud-Daulah, also known as the "Baby Taj," is a historic mausoleum located in Agra, India. This exquisite monument holds significant historical importance for several reasons. Following are the key points of tomb of itimad-ud-daulah:

1) **Mughal Era and Dynasty**:

The Tomb of Itimad-ud-Daulah was constructed during the Mughal era, which spanned from the early 16th to the mid-18th century in India. The Mughal dynasty, known for its cultural, architectural, and political contributions, left an indelible mark on Indian history. The tomb is a testament to this era's artistic and architectural achievements.

2) **Mirza Ghiyas Beg and His Role**:

   The tomb is the final resting place of Mirza Ghiyas Beg, a prominent Persian noble who played a pivotal role in the Mughal court. He held the title of Itimad-ud-Daulah, which translates to "Pillar of the State" or "Lord Treasurer." As the chief minister under Emperor Jahangir, his influence was profound, making his tomb historically significant.

3) **Chief Minister of Jahangir**:

   Mirza Ghiyas Beg served as the chief minister during the reign of Emperor Jahangir (1605–1627), one of the significant rulers of the Mughal dynasty. His role in the administration of the empire was instrumental in shaping Mughal policies and governance during this period.

4) **Political Influence**:

   As the chief minister, Mirza Ghiyas Beg played a crucial role in the political landscape of the Mughal Empire. His strategic decisions and advice influenced the policies and governance of the empire, impacting its stability and expansion.

5) **Economic Reforms**:

   Mirza Ghiyas Beg was renowned for his financial acumen. During his tenure as the treasurer (Itimad-ud-Daulah), he implemented several economic reforms that contributed to the financial stability of the empire. His contributions in this regard are historically significant, as they helped strengthen the Mughal economy.

6) **Family Legacy**:

   The tomb also serves as the final resting place for Mirza Ghiyas Beg's wife, Asmat Begum. This practice of commemorating both husband and wife in the same tomb is indicative of the Mughal tradition of preserving family legacies and expressing the importance of familial bonds.

7) **Architectural Transition**:

   The Tomb of Itimad-ud-Daulah is architecturally significant as it represents a transition in Mughal architectural styles. While earlier Mughal structures were predominantly constructed using red sandstone, this tomb showcases the growing preference for white marble, which would later become a hallmark of Mughal architecture.

8) **Architectural Inspiration**:

   Many architectural elements and design features of the Tomb of Itimad-ud-Daulah served as an inspiration for the construction of the Taj Mahal, the iconic Mughal monument built by Emperor Shah Jahan. The elegant use of white marble, symmetrical layout, and intricate carvings found in the tomb can be seen in the Taj

Mahal, highlighting its historical significance in influencing subsequent architectural masterpieces.

9) **Cultural Heritage**:
The tomb is an integral part of India's cultural heritage and represents the zenith of Mughal artistic and architectural achievements. Its inclusion as a UNESCO World Heritage Site underscores its cultural significance and the importance of preserving this historical treasure.

10) **Tourism and Education**:
The Tomb of Itimad-ud-Daulah has become a popular tourist destination, drawing visitors from around the world. It serves as an educational resource for students of architecture, history, and art, offering insights into the rich history and culture of the Mughal dynasty. Tourism also contributes to the preservation and maintenance of this historic site.

1.4 Qutub Minar:

The Qutub Minar, located in Delhi, India, is a magnificent UNESCO World Heritage Site and a remarkable example of Indo-Islamic architecture. Standing at a height of 73 meters (240 feet), it is the world's tallest brick minaret and has five distinct stories, each adorned with intricate carvings and inscriptions in Arabic and Nagari scripts. Built in the 12th century by Qutb-ud-din Aibak and later completed by Iltutmish, the Qutub Minar serves as a symbol of the city's rich historical and cultural heritage. It is surrounded by other historical structures and lush gardens, making it a popular destination for tourists and history enthusiasts, offering a glimpse into India's medieval architectural excellence and its complex history of rulers and dynasties.

1.4.1 Features of Qutub Minar:

Here are key features of the Qutub Minar:

1) **Historical Background**:
The Qutub Minar, constructed in the early 13th century, is a towering minaret that stands as a testament to India's rich history. It was built during the reign of Qutb-ud-din Aibak, the founder of the Delhi Sultanate, and later expanded and completed by his successor, Iltutmish.

2) **Architectural Style**:
The Qutub Minar showcases a blend of various architectural styles, primarily Indo-Islamic and Persian. Its unique design incorporates elements of Islamic art, including intricate calligraphy and geometric patterns, making it an exceptional example of early Indo-Islamic architecture in India.

3) **Tall and Sturdy Structure**:
The minaret stands at a remarkable height of 73 meters (240 feet) and consists of five distinct stories, each marked by projecting balconies (mehrab) and intricately

carved bands of Quranic inscriptions. Its impressive height and solid construction make it the tallest brick minaret in the world.

4) **Materials Used**:

The Qutub Minar is predominantly constructed from red sandstone and white marble. The use of these materials adds to the monument's visual appeal and ensures its durability. The white marble, in particular, is used for the intricately carved details and inscriptions.

5) **Calligraphic Inscriptions**:

The minaret is adorned with beautiful calligraphic inscriptions from the Quran and other Islamic texts. These inscriptions are finely carved in the Kufic script and serve both decorative and religious purposes, enhancing the cultural and artistic value of the monument.

6) **Architectural Elements**:

The Qutub Minar features a range of architectural elements, including fluted columns, projecting balconies with stalactite pendentives, and decorative bands. The balconies and bands are replete with intricate geometric and floral designs, showcasing the skill of the artisans of the time.

7) **Iron Pillar**:

Adjacent to the Qutub Minar stands the famous Iron Pillar of Delhi. This remarkable iron pillar, made of nearly pure wrought iron, has attracted scientific interest due to its rust-resistant properties and remarkable corrosion resistance over centuries. It is a testament to the metallurgical prowess of ancient India.

8) **Complex of Historical Structures**:

The Qutub Minar is part of a larger historical complex that includes several other significant structures, such as the Quwwat-ul-Islam Mosque, the Alai Darwaza, the Tomb of Iltutmish, and the Tomb of Imam Zamin. This complex reflects the historical and cultural diversity of the Delhi Sultanate.

9) **Cultural Significance**:

The Qutub Minar and its surrounding complex represent the rich cultural heritage of India and the architectural legacy of the Delhi Sultanate. It has been recognized as a UNESCO World Heritage Site, drawing visitors, historians, and architects from around the world who seek to explore its historical and artistic significance.

10) **Tourist Attraction**:

The Qutub Minar is a popular tourist destination in Delhi, attracting millions of visitors annually. Tourists come not only to admire its architectural grandeur but also to learn about its historical context, making it an educational and cultural hotspot in the heart of India's capital.

1.4.2 Historic Significance of Qutub Minar:

The Qutub Minar, located in Delhi, India, is a monument of immense historical significance. Its historical importance is rooted in several key aspects:

1) **Early Islamic Rule in India**:
   The construction of the Qutub Minar commenced in the late 12th century during the rule of Qutb-ud-din Aibak, the founder of the Delhi Sultanate. This marked the establishment of Islamic rule in northern India, which significantly influenced the region's history, culture, and architecture.

2) **Dynastic Transition**:
   Qutb-ud-din Aibak's completion of the Qutub Minar was continued by his successor, Iltutmish. This transition of power and the completion of the monument represent the consolidation of the Delhi Sultanate as a prominent dynasty in India, which would have a lasting impact on the country's history.

3) **Indo-Islamic Architecture**:
   The Qutub Minar is a prime example of early Indo-Islamic architecture in India. It showcases the fusion of Persian, Islamic, and Indian architectural styles, setting the stage for the development of distinct architectural traditions in the subcontinent.

4) **Architectural Innovations**:
   The Qutub Minar introduced architectural innovations in India, including the use of red sandstone and white marble, intricate calligraphy, and geometric designs. These features served as prototypes for later Islamic monuments in the region, leaving a lasting architectural legacy.

5) **Symbol of Triumph**:
   Historically, the Qutub Minar was built to commemorate the victory of Qutb-ud-din Aibak over the last Hindu kingdom in Delhi. Its construction symbolized the conquest and establishment of Muslim rule in northern India, which had a profound impact on the region's history.

6) **Cultural Interaction**:
   The Qutub Minar complex includes the Quwwat-ul-Islam Mosque, which incorporates elements from pre-existing Hindu and Jain temples. This cultural interaction and adaptation of existing structures into Islamic architecture illustrate the complex history of religious and cultural exchange in India.

7) **World Heritage Site**:
   The Qutub Minar complex, including the minaret, is recognized as a UNESCO World Heritage Site. This designation underscores its global historical and cultural significance, drawing attention to its architectural and historical value.

8) **Metallurgical Marvel**:
   The adjacent Iron Pillar of Delhi, dating back to the Gupta period (4th-5th century CE), is renowned for its exceptional rust resistance. This iron pillar has attracted

scientific interest due to its advanced metallurgical properties, representing ancient India's achievements in metallurgy and engineering.

9) **Delhi's Legacy**:
The Qutub Minar and its complex are integral to the historical narrative of Delhi, which has served as a capital for numerous dynasties, including the Delhi Sultanate, the Mughals, and the British. It represents Delhi's enduring significance as a center of political and cultural power.

10) **Tourist Attraction and Education**:
The Qutub Minar complex continues to be a major tourist attraction, drawing visitors from around the world who come to learn about India's rich history, architecture, and cultural diversity. It serves as an educational resource, providing insights into the region's historical and architectural evolution.

1.5 Alai Darwaza:

The Alai Darwaza, located in Delhi, India, is a historical gateway and architectural masterpiece constructed during the rule of Alauddin Khilji in the 14th century. It is celebrated for its unique architectural features, including a magnificent dome, intricate geometric patterns, and exquisite calligraphic inscriptions. The Alai Darwaza serves as a testament to the architectural prowess of the Delhi Sultanate and is recognized for its significant contribution to Indo-Islamic architecture. As one of the few remaining structures from the Khilji dynasty, it stands as a symbol of historical and cultural heritage, attracting visitors and historians alike to explore its artistic grandeur and historical relevance in India's capital.

1.5.1 Features of Alai Darwaza:

Here are ten key features and aspects of the Alai Darwaza:

1) **Architectural Style**:
The Alai Darwaza is a prime example of Indo-Islamic architecture, showcasing a fusion of Indian and Islamic design elements. It was built during the Khalji dynasty's rule in the 14th century, during the reign of Alauddin Khilji.

2) **Magnificent Dome**:
One of the most striking features of the Alai Darwaza is its large, imposing dome. This dome is constructed using intricately arranged geometric patterns and is supported by a series of concentric rings, creating a visually stunning architectural element.

3) **Intricate Carvings**:
The facade of the Alai Darwaza is adorned with intricate carvings and decorative elements. These carvings include geometric patterns, arabesque designs, and inscriptions from the Quran, adding to the monument's artistic beauty.

4) **Calligraphic Inscriptions**:
The Alai Darwaza features inscriptions in Arabic script that contain verses from the Quran. These calligraphic elements serve both decorative and religious purposes, reflecting the Islamic cultural influence on the architecture.

5) **Colossal Arches**:
The gateway is renowned for its colossal arched openings, which are framed by ornamental bands and decorative panels. These arches provide a sense of grandeur and signify the importance of the structure.

6) **Red Sandstone Construction**:
Similar to many historical monuments in Delhi, the Alai Darwaza is primarily constructed from red sandstone. The use of this durable material is characteristic of Indo-Islamic architecture and adds to the monument's longevity.

7) **Cultural Significance**:
The Alai Darwaza holds cultural significance as it represents the architectural achievements of the Khalji dynasty. It stands as a symbol of the era's cultural and artistic contributions to Delhi's historical landscape.

8) **Gateway to the Quwwat-ul-Islam Mosque**:
The Alai Darwaza originally served as the southern gateway to the Quwwat-ul-Islam Mosque, which was one of the earliest mosques built in India. It was constructed by repurposing materials from pre-existing Hindu and Jain temples, showcasing a blend of architectural influences.

9) **Historical Legacy**:
The Alai Darwaza is a testament to the reign of Alauddin Khilji, a powerful and influential ruler of the Delhi Sultanate. Its construction reflects the political and architectural ambitions of his time.

10) **Tourist Attraction**:
Today, the Alai Darwaza is a popular tourist attraction in Delhi, drawing visitors from around the world who come to admire its architectural beauty, learn about its historical significance, and explore the larger Qutub Minar complex, where it is located.

1.5.2 Historical Significance of Alai Darwaza:

The Alai Darwaza is a historically significant architectural marvel located in the Qutub Complex in Delhi, India. Built during the 14th century, this magnificent gateway holds immense historical, cultural, and architectural significance.

1) **Architectural Marvel of the Delhi Sultanate:**
The Alai Darwaza was constructed in 1311 CE during the reign of Alauddin Khilji, the second ruler of the Khilji dynasty in the Delhi Sultanate. It stands as a testament to the architectural prowess of the time.

2) **Innovative Design and Features:**

The Alai Darwaza showcases innovative architectural features, such as its true horseshoe-shaped arches and the use of red sandstone and white marble in its construction. These features were uncommon in India at the time and reflect the influence of Islamic architecture.

3) **Historical Context:**

The 14th century marked a period of significant political and cultural transformation in India. The Delhi Sultanate, under Alauddin Khilji's rule, was expanding its territories and consolidating its power.

4) **Symbol of Alauddin Khilji's Ambition:**

The construction of the Alai Darwaza was a symbol of Alauddin Khilji's ambition to surpass his predecessors in terms of architectural achievements. He sought to leave a lasting legacy through this grand gateway.

5) **Architectural Fusion:**

The Alai Darwaza represents a fusion of Indian and Islamic architectural styles. While its horseshoe arches are of Islamic origin, the use of red sandstone and intricate carvings reflects the Indian aesthetic.

6) **Use of Verses from the Quran:**

The gateway is adorned with intricate calligraphy, including verses from the Quran. This highlights the cultural and religious significance of the structure in the context of Islamic rule.

7) **Symbol of Power and Authority:**

The Alai Darwaza served as a symbol of the Sultan's authority and his ability to undertake grand architectural projects. It was not only a functional gate but also a statement of power.

8) **Role in the Qutub Complex:**

The Alai Darwaza is an integral part of the Qutub Complex, which includes the famous Qutub Minar. It stands at the southern entrance of the complex and enhances its grandeur.

9) **Preservation of History:**

The Alai Darwaza has survived centuries of natural disasters, invasions, and urban development. Its preservation has allowed us to connect with the rich history of the Delhi Sultanate.

10) **Historical Significance of Qutub Complex:**

The Qutub Complex, of which the Alai Darwaza is a part, is a UNESCO World Heritage Site. It represents the historical significance of the region as a center of power and culture.

11) Influence on Later Architecture:

The architectural innovations seen in the Alai Darwaza had a lasting impact on subsequent Islamic architecture in India. It set a precedent for the use of red sandstone and marble in monumental structures.

12) Cultural and Touristic Importance:

Today, the Alai Darwaza is a popular tourist attraction and a symbol of India's rich cultural heritage. It continues to draw visitors from around the world, contributing to the country's tourism industry.

♦♦♦

Review Questions

Q.1. Answer the Following Questions.

1) Explain the Techniques of Making Arches.
2) Discuss in detail about the Techniques of Making Domes.
3) Explain in detail about the Quwwat-ul-Islam Masjid.
4) Explain the Features of Tomb of Iltumis
4) Explain in detail about the Historical Significance of Tomb of Iltumis.
5) Discuss about the Features of Qutub Minar.
6) Explain the Historical Significance of Qutub Minar.
7) Explain in detail Features of Alai Darwaza
8) Discuss about the Historical Significance of Alai Darwaza.

Q.3. Write Short Notes on:

1) Techniques of Making Arches.
2) Techniques of Making Dome.
2) Quwwat-ul-Islam Masjid.
4) Tomb of Iltumis.
5) Qutub Minar.
6) Alai Darwaza.

♦♦♦

UNIT 2

Emergence and Development of Deccan Art & Architecture

2.1 Bahamani

2.2 Vijaynagar

2.3 Maratha

Introduction:

The emergence and development of Deccan art and architecture represent a fascinating journey through time, encompassing diverse dynasties, cultural influences, and artistic innovations across the Deccan Plateau in South India. Beginning with the early cave temples at Ajanta and Ellora in the 2nd century BCE, Deccan art bore witness to the integration of indigenous and foreign elements, notably the architectural and artistic influences of Buddhist, Jain, and Hindu traditions. Over centuries, the Chalukyas, Rashtrakutas, Hoysalas, and Kakatiyas, among others, played pivotal roles in shaping Deccan architecture. The monumental rock-cut temples at Badami, Aihole, and Pattadakal exemplify the fusion of Dravidian and Nagara styles, showcasing intricate sculptures and temple layouts that have left an indelible mark on Indian architecture. However, the zenith of Deccan art and architecture is perhaps epitomized by the Kakatiya dynasty's exquisite Kakatiya temples, particularly the Ramappa Temple, renowned for its intricate carvings and floating bricks, and the magnificent Hoysala temples, such as the Chennakesava Temple at Belur, with its intricate friezes and delicate sculptures. During the Bahmani and Vijayanagara periods, Islamic and Persian influences began to meld with the existing Dravidian and Nagara styles, resulting in unique structures like the Gol Gumbaz, the largest dome in India, and the stunning Hampi temples. This rich amalgamation of styles reached its apogee with the Qutb Shahi dynasty's Golconda Fort and Charminar, characterized by their intricate stucco work and Indo-Islamic architectural elements. Furthermore, the Mughal conquest of the Deccan brought forth a new chapter in the region's architectural history, with structures like the Bibi Ka Maqbara in Aurangabad, often referred to as the 'Mini Taj,' showcasing the Mughal aesthetic in a Deccani context. The distinctiveness of Deccan art and architecture lies in its ability to continually adapt and integrate diverse influences, resulting in a unique blend of artistic expression that mirrors the region's vibrant cultural tapestry and historical evolution.

2.1 Bahamani:

The Bahmani Sultanate, established in 1347 CE in the Deccan region of South India, was a significant medieval Indian kingdom known for its cultural diversity, administrative innovation, and architectural splendor. It emerged as an independent power, breaking away from the weakening Delhi Sultanate, and its administration featured influential officials like the Wazir and Diwan-i-Arz, while its revenue system relied on land taxation. The Bahmani Sultanate promoted religious tolerance, fostered cultural exchanges, and patronized art and literature, leading to the creation of exquisite architectural marvels such as the Gulbarga Fort and the Madrasa of Mahmud Gawan. Despite its eventual fragmentation into the Deccan Sultanates, the Bahmani Sultanate's legacy endures as a testament to the rich tapestry of medieval Indian history.

2.1.1 Arts in Bahamani Sultanate:

The Bahmani Sultanate, which ruled over the Deccan region of India from the early 14th century to the late 15th century, was a dynamic and culturally diverse empire that made significant contributions to various forms of art and culture. This period was characterized by a rich blend of Islamic, Persian, and indigenous Deccani influences, resulting in a unique artistic heritage that included architecture, calligraphy, painting, music, literature, coinage, textiles, and more. The arts in the Bahmani Sultanate played a crucial role in shaping the cultural landscape of the Deccan and left a lasting impact on subsequent dynasties in the region.

A) Emergence of Art during Bahamani Period:

The Bahmani Sultanate, which ruled over the Deccan region of India from the early 14th century to the late 15th century, witnessed the emergence of a rich and diverse artistic tradition. The art during the Bahmani period was characterized by its patronage of various art forms, especially in the realms of architecture, calligraphy, and manuscript illumination. This period marked a confluence of diverse influences, resulting in a unique artistic style that reflected the cosmopolitan nature of the Bahmani Sultanate.

1) Architectural Patronage:

The Bahamani Sultanate was known for its significant patronage of art and architecture. The rulers recognized the importance of these forms of expression for showcasing their authority and cultural identity. Bahamani architecture was characterized by a fusion of diverse influences, including Islamic, Persian, and indigenous Indian styles. This amalgamation created a unique and cosmopolitan architectural tradition.

2) **Deccani Style:**

The Bahmani period marked the emergence of the Deccani style, which became a hallmark of the region. This style was a unique blend of different cultural elements and artistic traditions. Deccani architecture featured bulbous domes, pointed arches, and intricate stonework. These elements combined to create a distinctive regional architectural style that reflected the cultural diversity of the Deccan plateau.

3) **Architectural Characteristics:**

Bulbous Domes: Bahmani architecture prominently featured bulbous domes, often large and intricately designed. These domes added grandeur and aesthetic appeal to the structures. They became a signature feature of Deccani architecture. Pointed Arches: The use of pointed arches was another key characteristic, reflecting Islamic architectural influences. These arches provided both structural stability and visual elegance, contributing to the overall beauty of the buildings. Intricate Stonework: Deccani craftsmen were skilled in intricate stonework, including ornate carvings and delicate latticework. This craftsmanship adorned the facades, doorways, and minarets of architectural structures.

4) **Gol Gumbaz:**

Gol Gumbaz, located in Bijapur, stands as one of the most iconic architectural achievements of the Bahmani period. Built by Sultan Muhammad Adil Shah, it features one of the world's largest unsupported domes. The Gol Gumbaz is renowned for its massive dome, intricate gallery, and four minarets, all of which showcase the architectural prowess of the time.

5) **Mausoleums and Tombs:**

Mausoleums and tombs played a significant role in Bahmani art and architecture. These structures were erected to honor rulers, nobles, and other dignitaries, combining elements of Persian and Islamic funerary architecture with indigenous Indian influences. Notable examples include the Ibrahim Rauza in Bijapur, celebrated for its symmetrical design, elegant minarets, and exquisite façade ornamentation.

6) **Calligraphy and Ornamentation:**

Calligraphy was a vital aspect of Bahmani art, with inscriptions in Arabic script adorning many architectural structures. These inscriptions often conveyed religious verses, royal decrees, or poetic verses, adding a spiritual and aesthetic dimension to the architecture. The intricate ornamentation and decorative elements further enhanced the beauty of Bahmani architectural structures.

7) **Cultural Significance:**

The emergence of art during the Bahmani period was not only a reflection of artistic achievements but also a testament to the cultural diversity and cosmopolitan nature of the Bahmani Sultanate. The architectural legacy of the Bahmani period continues to be celebrated for its unique blend of cultural influences and its enduring impact on the Deccan region's artistic heritage.

B) Development of Art Forms during Bahamani Period:

The Bahmani Sultanate in the Deccan region of India witnessed the patronage and development of various art forms during its rule. Some of the major art forms that flourished during the Bahmani period include:

1) Indo-Persian Architecture:

Bahmani architecture was a fusion of Persian and indigenous Indian styles. This architectural form featured elements like arches, domes, minarets, and large courtyards. Prominent examples include the Gol Gumbaz in Bijapur and the Bidar Fort.

2) Calligraphy:

Persian and Arabic calligraphy was extensively used in the decoration of buildings and manuscripts. Inscriptions in beautiful calligraphy adorned mosques, tombs, and other structures, adding an artistic and religious dimension to them.

3) Jali Work:

The use of jali, or intricately carved stone latticework, was a prominent feature in Bahmani architecture. These screens allowed for the interplay of light and shadow and added a sense of elegance to buildings like mosques and tombs.

4) Geometric Patterns and Floral Motifs:

Geometric patterns and intricate floral motifs were commonly used as decorative elements in architecture, textiles, and manuscripts. These designs reflected the influence of Islamic art, with its emphasis on geometric patterns and representations of nature.

5) Manuscript Illumination:

Persian miniature painting styles influenced the art of manuscript illustration during the Bahmani period. Manuscripts and literary works were adorned with colourful illustrations and intricate details.

6) Ceramics and Pottery:

Ceramics and pottery production thrived during the Bahmani period. These items were known for their intricate designs and vibrant glazes. The Bahmani region also saw the rise of Bidriware, a type of metalwork with silver or brass inlay on blackened metal.

7) Tile Decoration:

Decorative tiles were used to embellish the facades of buildings in some Bahmani regions, particularly Bidar. These tiles featured vibrant colors and intricate patterns.

8) Textile and Carpet Weaving:

Fine textiles and carpets were produced during the Bahmani period. These textiles often featured intricate designs and were known for their use of natural dyes. The production of high-quality textiles was a significant economic activity in the Bahmani Sultanate.

9) **Woodwork:**
Woodwork was another important art form. Carved wooden elements adorned palaces, mosques, and other structures. The intricate designs on wooden screens and panels showcased the skill of Bahmani artisans.

10) **Metalwork:**
Besides Bidriware, which is a distinctive form of metalwork with intricate inlay patterns on metal objects, metalwork was used for the creation of ornate doors, lamps, and other decorative items.

11) **Cultural Exchange:**
The Bahmani Sultanate was a melting pot of cultures due to its strategic location in the Deccan plateau. This led to a rich cultural exchange, resulting in the fusion of artistic styles from various regions.

12) **Carpentry:**
Carpentry was an essential aspect of architectural and artistic construction. Woodworkers crafted intricate designs for doors, screens, and ceilings, enhancing the aesthetics of buildings.

13) **Embroidery and Textile Arts:**
The Deccan region was known for its textile arts, including intricate embroidery and embellishments on clothing and textiles.

14) **Ivory Carving:**
Ivory carving was a notable art form, producing exquisite pieces like figurines, boxes, and jewellery.

15) **Potpourri of Influences:**
The art forms of the Bahmani period were characterized by a potpourri of influences, including Persian, Central Asian, and indigenous Indian styles. This blending of artistic traditions resulted in a unique and distinctive cultural and artistic legacy.

C) **Importance of Bahamani Art:**
Art during the Bahmani Sultanate period in the Deccan region of India holds significant historical, cultural, and artistic importance for several reasons:

1) **Cultural Synthesis:**
The Bahmani Sultanate was located at the crossroads of various cultural and artistic influences. As a result, the art of this period represents a rich and unique synthesis of Persian, Central Asian, and indigenous Indian artistic traditions. This cultural fusion is a testament to the cosmopolitan nature of the Deccan.

2) **Architectural Marvels:**
Bahmani architecture produced iconic structures that continue to stand as architectural marvels. The Gol Gumbaz in Bijapur, with the world's second-largest

dome, and the intricately designed Bidar Fort are notable examples. These buildings showcase the excellence of Indo-Persian architectural styles and techniques.

3) **Calligraphic Excellence:**

The extensive use of Persian and Arabic calligraphy in Bahmani art is a testament to the high regard for the written word and religious inscriptions. Calligraphy added aesthetic and spiritual value to the structures, reflecting the cultural significance of writing in Islamic art.

4) **Cultural Exchange:**

The Bahmani Sultanate's strategic location facilitated cultural exchanges between different regions. This exchange of ideas, artistic techniques, and traditions led to a unique artistic heritage that is distinct from both northern and southern Indian art.

5) **Innovation in Architecture:**

The Bahmani period saw the development of innovative architectural features, such as the use of jali (latticework) screens, which created stunning visual effects through the interplay of light and shadow. These architectural innovations continue to inspire modern architects.

6) **Influence on Later Dynasties:**

The artistic and architectural innovations of the Bahmani period had a lasting impact on later dynasties in the Deccan, such as the Adil Shahi and Qutb Shahi dynasties. Their artistic and architectural styles bear the influence of the Bahmani Sultanate.

7) **Contribution to Bidriware:**

The Bahmani Sultanate is credited with the development of Bidriware, a unique form of metalwork that involves inlaying silver or brass on blackened metal. This art form continues to be highly regarded and is associated with the region.

8) **Historical Significance:**

The art and architecture of the Bahmani Sultanate reflect the historical and political importance of the Deccan during this period. They are a testament to the power, wealth, and cultural achievements of the Bahmani rulers.

9) **Cultural Heritage:**

The art and cultural expressions of the Bahmani period are an integral part of the cultural heritage of the Deccan region and continue to be celebrated through various cultural events and heritage preservation efforts.

10) **Aesthetic Beauty:**

The art and architecture of the Bahmani period are celebrated for their aesthetic beauty and elegance. They continue to captivate art enthusiasts, historians, and tourists alike, contributing to the cultural richness of the Deccan.

11) Preservation of History:

These artistic and architectural monuments serve as historical records, providing insights into the socio-political and cultural context of the Bahmani Sultanate and the Deccan region during this period.

12) Educational and Research Value:

Bahmani art serves as a subject of study and research in art history, archaeology, and architectural history. It contributes to our understanding of the artistic development of the Deccan and its historical significance.

2.1.2 Architecture in Bahamani Sultanate:

The architecture of the Bahamani Sultanate, which thrived in the Deccan region of India from the early 14th century to the late 15th century, is a testament to the artistic and cultural achievements of the dynasty. The sultans of the Bahamani Sultanate were great patrons of architecture, and their architectural legacy is a reflection of the diverse cultural influences and unique stylistic elements that characterized the Deccan during this period.

A) Emergence of Architecture During Bahamani Period:

The Bahmani Sultanate, which existed in the Deccan region of India from the 14th to the 16th century, played a pivotal role in the emergence of a unique architectural tradition characterized by its Indo-Persian fusion. The emergence of architecture during the Bahmani period is noteworthy for several key developments:

1) Indo-Persian Architectural Synthesis:

The Bahmani architecture was marked by the fusion of indigenous Indian and Persian architectural elements. This synthesis led to the creation of a distinctive architectural style that combined the use of arches and domes from Persian architecture with indigenous Indian designs.

2) Grand Fortifications:

The Bahmani rulers constructed massive forts and citadels, which often featured impressive gateways, bastions, and fortified walls. These structures served as symbols of the rulers' authority and power. Notable examples include the Bidar Fort and the Gulbarga Fort.

3) Mosques and Religious Buildings:

Mosques were integral to Bahmani architecture. These religious structures were characterized by large prayer halls, towering minarets, and exquisite stucco work. The Jami Masjid in Gulbarga and the Rauza-e-Ala in Bidar are fine specimens of mosque architecture.

4) Stellate Architecture:

The Bahmani period is renowned for its use of the stellate (star-shaped) architectural plan in temple complexes. This unique design featured a central courtyard from which multiple structures radiated, creating a visually captivating layout.

5) **Intricately Carved Stone Structures:**
Bahmani architecture prominently featured intricately carved stone structures. These carvings adorned the exteriors and interiors of buildings, showcasing a high level of craftsmanship. The designs often depicted scenes from Hindu epics and Islamic art.

6) **Arches and Domes:**
The use of pointed arches and domes was a distinct feature of Bahmani architecture. These architectural elements added grace and grandeur to the structures and were influenced by Persian architectural traditions.

7) **Calligraphy and Inscriptions:**
Persian and Arabic calligraphy was commonly employed for inscriptions on buildings. These inscriptions were not only aesthetically pleasing but also conveyed religious messages, praises, and other forms of expression.

8) **Jali Work:**
The use of jali, or intricately carved stone latticework, was prevalent in Bahmani architecture. These screens allowed for the interplay of light and shadow, creating a visually captivating effect in buildings such as mosques and tombs.

9) **Utilization of Local Materials:**
Bahmani architecture often utilized locally available materials, such as stone and stucco. This practice contributed to the distinctive architectural style of the Deccan region.

10) **Hindu and Buddhist Influence:**
The Bahmani period witnessed the construction of Hindu and Buddhist religious structures that incorporated elements of Islamic and indigenous architectural styles. The Kali Masjid and the Chauk Masjid in Bidar are examples of this synthesis.

11) **Continued Influence:**
The architectural innovations of the Bahmani period left a lasting impact on later dynasties in the Deccan, such as the Adil Shahi and Qutb Shahi dynasties. The architectural styles developed during the Bahmani period continued to influence the region's later architectural endeavors.

12) **Cultural Diversity:**
Bahmani architecture reflected the empire's cultural and religious diversity. Buildings were constructed for various religious communities, showcasing the empire's policy of religious tolerance and cultural inclusivity.

B) Development of Architecture During Bahamani Period:

The Bahmani Sultanate, a medieval Deccan sultanate that existed from the 14th to the 16th century, made significant contributions to the development of architecture in the Deccan region of India. The architecture during the Bahmani period is known for its synthesis of various influences, including Persian, Indian, and Islamic styles. Here's an overview of the development of architecture during the Bahmani period:

1) **Indo-Persian Architectural Synthesis:**

One of the distinguishing features of Bahmani architecture was its Indo-Persian architectural synthesis. It combined elements of Persian architecture, such as arches and domes, with indigenous Indian architectural styles, creating a unique and distinct architectural tradition.

2) **Majestic Forts and Palaces:**

The Bahmani rulers constructed imposing forts and palaces as symbols of their power and authority. These structures often featured massive walls, impressive gateways, and ornate arches. Examples include the Bidar Fort and the fortifications at Gulbarga.

3) **Mosques and Religious Buildings:**

Bahmani rulers commissioned the construction of mosques and religious buildings, often marked by large prayer halls, minarets, and exquisite stucco work. The Jami Masjid in Gulbarga and the Rauza-e-Ala in Bidar are noteworthy examples of mosque architecture.

4) **Stellate Architecture:**

The Bahmani period is known for its use of the stellate (star-shaped) architectural plan, particularly in temple complexes. This unique layout featured a central courtyard with multiple structures radiating outward, creating an aesthetically pleasing design.

5) **Carved Stone Structures:**

Bahmani architecture was characterized by intricately carved stone structures. The use of stone allowed for intricate designs and relief work, which adorned many buildings, including temples, palaces, and mosques.

6) **Arches and Domes:**

The Bahmani architecture prominently featured pointed arches and domes, which were borrowed from Persian architectural traditions. These elements added elegance and grandeur to the structures.

7) **Calligraphy and Inscriptions:**

Persian and Arabic calligraphy was commonly used for inscriptions on buildings, adding a sense of aesthetic and spiritual significance to the architecture. These inscriptions often conveyed religious messages and praises.

8) **Jali Work:**

The use of jali, or intricately carved stone latticework, was prevalent in Bahmani architecture. These screens allowed for the play of light and shadow, creating a visually captivating effect in buildings like mosques and tombs.

9) Use of Local Materials:

Bahmani architecture often made use of local materials like stone and stucco. This incorporation of regional resources contributed to the distinctive architectural style of the Deccan.

10) Stupas and Temples:

The Bahmani period saw the construction of stupas and Hindu temples. These structures showcased a blend of Islamic and indigenous architectural elements. The Kali Masjid and the Chauk Masjid in Bidar exemplify this fusion.

11) Influence on Later Dynasties:

The architectural innovations of the Bahmani period had a lasting impact on later dynasties in the Deccan, including the Adil Shahi and Qutb Shahi dynasties. The architectural styles developed during the Bahmani period continued to influence the region's subsequent architecture.

12) Cultural and Religious Tolerance:

The architecture of the Bahmani period reflected the empire's cultural and religious diversity. Buildings were constructed for various religious and cultural communities, reflecting the empire's policy of religious tolerance.

C) Importance of Bahamani Architecture:

The architectural legacy of the Bahmani Sultanate, which existed from the 14th to the 16th centuries in the Deccan region of India, holds immense importance due to its historical, cultural, and architectural significance. The Bahmani architecture, characterized by its fusion of Islamic, Persian, and indigenous Indian elements, has left an indelible mark on the region's heritage and continues to be a subject of scholarly study and cultural pride.

1) Historical Significance:

The Bahmani Sultanate, founded by Alauddin Bahman Shah in 1347, played a pivotal role in the political and cultural landscape of the Deccan. Its architectural achievements reflect the historical context of the time. The Bahmani Sultanate emerged during a period of significant political change, as it sought to establish itself as an independent and powerful entity in the Deccan region. The architecture of the Bahmani period serves as a tangible testament to this historical transformation, encapsulating the dynastic ambitions and achievements of the sultans and nobility who ruled during this time.

2) Cultural Syncretism

Bahmani architecture is celebrated for its unique blend of Islamic, Persian, and indigenous Indian architectural elements. This fusion reflects the cultural diversity and syncretism of the Deccan region, which was a melting pot of various ethnicities, religions, and artistic traditions. The architecture of the Bahmani period serves as a manifestation of this cultural integration, demonstrating how different artistic and architectural influences were harmoniously combined. This syncretic approach is not only a testament to the cultural richness of the Deccan but also serves as an inspiration for contemporary ideas of inclusivity and cultural exchange.

3) **Architectural Innovation:**
The Bahmani period witnessed significant architectural innovation, contributing to the broader trajectory of Indian architecture. The architects of the time developed distinctive architectural features and styles, such as the bulbous domes and corbelled arches. These innovations not only reflected the aesthetic tastes of the period but also influenced later architectural developments in the Deccan and beyond. The bulbous domes, in particular, became a hallmark of Bahmani architecture and continued to be a prominent feature in the architecture of subsequent dynasties like the Adil Shahi and Qutb Shahi.

4) **Commemorative Structures:**
The architecture of the Bahmani period features numerous commemorative structures, including tombs and mosques, built to honor rulers, nobles, and other prominent individuals. These buildings were not merely functional but also carried significant historical and cultural weight. They served as markers of power, prestige, and remembrance. The grandeur of these structures and the intricate ornamentation on their facades are a testament to the importance of commemorating key figures in the Deccan's history.

5) **Influence on Subsequent Styles:**
Bahmani architecture had a profound influence on later architectural styles in the Deccan. The fusion of various elements, as seen in the Bahmani period, continued to shape the architectural traditions of the region, notably in the Adil Shahi and Qutb Shahi periods. The bulbous domes, corbelled arches, and other architectural innovations introduced during the Bahmani Sultanate became enduring features in the architectural vocabulary of the Deccan. This influence also extended to other parts of India, as architectural ideas and styles often traveled and adapted to different regions.

6) **Water Management and Engineering:**
The Bahmani Sultanate's location in the arid Deccan region necessitated innovative water management solutions. The construction of stepwells and tanks, characterized by their intricate geometric patterns and architectural features, highlighted the importance of efficient water management. These structures not only served practical purposes but also demonstrated the architectural ingenuity required to address the water needs of the region. They stand as a testament to the technological advancements of the period.

7) **Syncretic Architectural Styles:**
The architecture of the Bahmani Sultanate represents the syncretism of cultural and artistic influences. It exemplifies the harmonious blending of Persian, Islamic, and

Indian elements, showing the cultural integration and tolerance that characterized the Deccan. This syncretic approach underscores the importance of cross-cultural interactions and their impact on art and architecture.

8) **Preservation of Heritage:**

Many architectural structures from the Bahmani period have been preserved and maintained, serving as historical landmarks today. These buildings play a crucial role in preserving the cultural and architectural heritage of the Deccan. They offer a window into the past, allowing visitors to connect with the history and artistry of the Bahmani period. Preservation efforts underscore the importance of safeguarding architectural treasures for future generations.

9) **Cultural Identity and Pride:**

The architectural forms of the Bahmani period continue to be a source of cultural pride and identity for the Deccan region. They symbolize the historical legacy and artistic achievements of the Bahmani Sultanate. The distinct architectural elements, such as bulbous domes and decorative stucco work, serve as symbols of regional identity and are celebrated in local culture and traditions.

10) **Tourism and Cultural Heritage:**

Bahmani architecture attracts tourists and enthusiasts from around the world. The historical sites and architectural wonders of the Bahmani period contribute to tourism in the Deccan region, promoting economic growth and providing educational and cultural experiences. The preservation and promotion of these architectural treasures help maintain a connection to the region's rich cultural heritage.

11) **Architectural Diversity:**

The Bahmani Sultanate's architectural forms are known for their diversity and complexity. From grand mosques to imposing forts, from stepwells to exquisite tombs, the Bahmani architecture showcases a wide range of structures and styles. This diversity provides a holistic view of the architectural accomplishments of the period and adds to its historical and cultural significance.

12) **Artistic Expression:**

Bahmani architecture is a testament to the artistic expression and craftsmanship of the time. The intricacy of stucco work, the calligraphic embellishments, and the geometric designs on building facades and interiors reflect the skill and creativity of the artisans and craftsmen who contributed to these architectural marvels.

13) **Cultural Continuity:**

The architectural legacy of the Bahmani period is a bridge between the past and the present. It represents the continuity of cultural traditions and artistic practices in the Deccan region. The appreciation and study of Bahmani architecture help maintain a connection to the region's historical roots.

2.2 Vijaynagar:

Vijayanagara, founded in the 14th century in the Deccan Plateau of South India, was a magnificent Hindu empire known for its grandeur and cultural richness. Established by Harihara I and Bukka Raya I, the empire flourished under the reign of Krishnadevaraya and became a stronghold of Hinduism and culture, with remarkable architectural achievements like the Virupaksha Temple and the city of Hampi. Vijayanagara served as a formidable counterbalance to the Bahmani Sultanate and played a significant role in shaping the history of medieval South India until its decline following the Battle of Talikota in 1565, which marked the end of its glory but left an enduring legacy in art, architecture, and South Indian culture.

2.2.1 Arts in Vijaynagar Empire:

The Vijayanagara Empire, which thrived in Southern India from the 14th to the 17th century, was renowned for its rich and vibrant artistic and cultural heritage. The empire, centered around the capital city of Vijayanagara (modern-day Hampi), patronized various art forms, including architecture, sculpture, painting, and literature. The arts in the Vijayanagara Empire played a significant role in shaping the region's cultural identity and continue to be celebrated for their beauty and historical importance.

A) Emergence of Art During Vijaynagar Empire:

The emergence of art during the Vijayanagara Empire, which existed from the 14th to the 17th century in South India, marked a significant period of artistic and architectural excellence. The empire, known for its patronage of the arts, produced a rich and diverse range of artistic expressions. Here's an overview of the emergence of art during the Vijayanagara Empire:

1) Architectural Marvels:

The Vijayanagara rulers were renowned for their grand architectural projects. The capital city, Vijayanagara (Hampi), was home to numerous temples, palaces, and administrative buildings. The most famous among these is the Virupaksha Temple, which is still in use today. The architecture was characterized by large courtyards, tall gopurams (temple towers), and intricately carved stone structures.

2) Religious Art:

The empire was a stronghold of Hinduism, and religious art played a central role. Temples dedicated to various deities were constructed with exquisite sculptures and intricate carvings that depicted scenes from Hindu epics like the Ramayana and the Mahabharata. The Vittala Temple, with its iconic stone chariot and musical pillars, is a prime example of this religious art.

3) Monumental Temples:

The Vijayanagara rulers commissioned the construction of monumental temples, showcasing their devotion to Hindu deities. These temples featured towering gopurams adorned with intricate sculptures and relief work. The Hazara Rama Temple, the Vitthala Temple, and the Virupaksha Temple are notable examples.

4) **Secular Architecture:**

In addition to religious structures, the Vijayanagara Empire built secular buildings like palaces and fortifications. The Lotus Mahal, an ornate palace, and the Queen's Bath, with its Indo-Islamic architectural influence, are examples of the secular architectural excellence of the period.

5) **Stellate Plan:**

The Vijayanagara architecture is known for its unique stellate (star-shaped) plan, a distinct feature of several temple complexes. This architectural innovation allowed for a central courtyard with multiple structures radiating outward.

6) **Mysore Style of Architecture:**

The Vijayanagara Empire contributed to the development of the Mysore style of architecture, characterized by the use of large stone blocks, well-defined and massive pyramidal towers, and prominent pillars. This style had a significant influence on later temple architecture in South India.

7) **Bronze Sculptures:**

The empire excelled in the creation of bronze sculptures, particularly of deities. These sculptures showcased exquisite details and mastery of metallurgy. The bronze idol of Nataraja (Lord Shiva in the cosmic dance form) is one of the most famous examples.

8) **Mural Paintings:**

The Vijayanagara period also witnessed the creation of mural paintings in temple complexes. These paintings, typically found on the ceilings of temple corridors, depicted various themes, including mythological stories and daily life.

9) **Urban Planning:**

The capital city of Vijayanagara, with its well-planned streets, markets, and water infrastructure, reflected the empire's expertise in urban planning and architecture. The Hampi Bazaar, Virupaksha Bazaar, and the system of tanks and canals are testimonies to this.

10) **Cultural Patronage:**

The Vijayanagara rulers were great patrons of arts and culture. They provided support for poets, scholars, musicians, and dancers, contributing to the flourishing of literary and performing arts during the period.

11) **Legacy:**

The artistic and architectural legacy of the Vijayanagara Empire has left an indelible mark on South Indian art and culture. Many of the architectural and artistic elements developed during this period continued to influence later dynasties and are celebrated as a part of India's cultural heritage.

B) Development of Art During Vijaynagar Empire:

The Vijayanagara Empire, which thrived in South India from the 14th to the 17th century, was a prominent cultural and artistic center in Indian history. The period witnessed the flourishing of various art forms that reflected the rich socio-cultural milieu of the empire. This essay will delve into the major art forms that emerged and flourished during the Vijayanagara Empire, providing insights into their characteristics, significance, and enduring legacy.

1) Architecture:

One of the most distinctive features of the Vijayanagara Empire was its monumental architecture. The empire's architects blended indigenous Dravidian styles with elements of Islamic architecture, resulting in a unique architectural tradition. Notable examples include the Virupaksha Temple and the Vittala Temple in Hampi, both dedicated to Lord Shiva. These temples are characterized by their grand scale, intricate carvings, and ornate pillars. The Raya Gopurams, towering entrance gateways adorned with intricate sculptures, were another hallmark of Vijayanagara architecture. The architectural marvels of the empire stand as a testament to the skilled craftsmanship and aesthetic sensibilities of the period.

2) Sculpture:

Sculpture was another major art form that thrived during the Vijayanagara period. Skilled sculptors crafted exquisite sculptures of gods, goddesses, and mythological figures, which adorned temples and public spaces. The sculptures exhibited a high level of detail, depicting deities in various postures and expressions. Notable examples include the monolithic statue of Lord Ganesha at Hampi and the various panels depicting scenes from Hindu epics like the Ramayana and Mahabharata. The artistic finesse and religious devotion evident in Vijayanagara sculptures continue to captivate art enthusiasts and scholars alike.

3) Painting:

Though fewer examples of painting from the Vijayanagara period have survived compared to architecture and sculpture, the empire did have a vibrant tradition of mural paintings. The frescoes at the Lepakshi Veerabhadra Temple, for instance, showcase the use of vibrant colors and intricate detailing. These paintings depicted scenes from Hindu mythology, including stories of gods, goddesses, and legendary heroes. The art form provided a visual narrative that complemented the religious and cultural practices of the time.

4) Literature:

While not a visual art form, literature played a crucial role in the cultural landscape of the Vijayanagara Empire. The period witnessed a flowering of literary activity in various languages, including Sanskrit, Telugu, Kannada, and Tamil. Notable literary figures like Vemana, Annamacharya, and Krishnadevaraya himself were prolific poets and scholars. They composed devotional hymns, epic poetry, and scholarly treatises that celebrated the spiritual and cultural ethos of the empire.

5) Dance and Music:

The Vijayanagara period also saw a renaissance in the performing arts. Dance and music were integral parts of the cultural fabric. The empire patronized various forms of classical dance, including Bharatanatyam, Kuchipudi, and Odissi. Court musicians and dancers were highly regarded, and their performances were an essential component of royal ceremonies and public festivals. The compositions of the great saint-composer Purandaradasa exemplify the fusion of music, devotion, and cultural expression during this period.

6) Fortification and Urban Planning:

In addition to the traditional art forms, the architectural achievements of the Vijayanagara Empire extended to fortifications and urban planning. The capital city of Vijayanagara, Hampi, was a marvel of urban design, featuring well-planned streets, markets, and water supply systems. The city was strategically fortified with walls, watchtowers, and military structures, reflecting the empire's military prowess and administrative acumen.

C) Importance of Vijaynagar Empire in Arts:

The Vijayanagara Empire, which thrived in South India from the 14th to the 17th century, holds immense significance in the realm of arts and culture. This period was characterized by a flourishing of artistic endeavors across various domains, making it a pivotal chapter in the annals of Indian art and heritage. The importance of the Vijayanagara Empire in the arts can be understood by delving into its contributions to architecture, sculpture, painting, literature, and performing arts.

1) Architectural Marvels:

One of the most notable and enduring legacies of the Vijayanagara Empire is its architectural grandeur. The empire's architects and builders created monumental structures that continue to amaze and inspire to this day. Vijayanagara architecture is characterized by its distinctive blend of indigenous Dravidian styles with elements of Islamic architecture. This fusion resulted in a unique architectural tradition characterized by grand scale, intricate carvings, and ornate pillars. Notable examples include the Virupaksha Temple, dedicated to Lord Shiva, and the Vittala Temple, dedicated to Lord Vishnu, both located in Hampi. These temples are renowned for their towering entrance gateways known as Raya Gopurams, which are adorned with intricate sculptures and serve as iconic landmarks. The architectural innovations of the Vijayanagara Empire had a profound and lasting impact on subsequent South Indian temple architecture. The style and design principles developed during this period continue to influence architectural practices and temple construction in the region.

2) **Sculptural Excellence:**

Sculpture was another major art form that reached its zenith during the Vijayanagara Empire. The empire's skilled sculptors created exquisite sculptures of gods, goddesses, and mythological figures. These sculptures adorned temples, public spaces, and palaces. The sculptures are known for their precision, attention to detail, and the artist's deep devotion to the subject matter. Many of the sculptures depicted scenes from Hindu epics like the Ramayana and Mahabharata, as well as stories of various gods and goddesses. These sculptures served as a medium for religious and cultural storytelling, reinforcing the empire's spiritual and cultural values. The sculptural legacy of the Vijayanagara Empire continues to captivate art enthusiasts and scholars alike. It is a repository of South Indian religious and cultural heritage, providing insights into the artistic and religious sensibilities of the time.

3) **Fresco Paintings:**

While painting during the Vijayanagara period is not as extensively documented as other art forms, frescoes at sites like the Lepakshi Veerabhadra Temple provide valuable insights into the empire's contributions to this medium. The frescoes at Lepakshi Veerabhadra Temple employ vibrant colors and intricate detailing, enhancing their visual appeal. They predominantly depict scenes from Hindu mythology, which not only enriched the cultural experience for temple visitors but also conveyed moral and spiritual lessons. These frescoes served as a visual narrative, educating the largely illiterate populace about religious stories and cultural traditions. They played a significant role in conveying the rich tapestry of Hindu mythology and history.

4) **Literary Contributions:**

While literature is not a visual art form, it played a pivotal role in the cultural landscape of the Vijayanagara Empire. The period witnessed a flourishing of literary activity in various languages, including Sanskrit, Telugu, Kannada, and Tamil. Prolific poets and scholars like Vemana, Annamacharya, and Krishnadevaraya produced a vast body of work, including devotional hymns, epic poetry, and scholarly treatises. Vijayanagara literature celebrated the spiritual and cultural ethos of the empire. It preserved and propagated the values, beliefs, and stories of the time, contributing to the collective cultural memory of South India. Many literary works from this period continue to influence and inspire contemporary literature, particularly in the southern regions of India. The writings of Vijayanagara poets and scholars have left an indelible mark on the literary heritage of the subcontinent.

5) **Dance and Music:**

The Vijayanagara Empire played a pivotal role in the renaissance of the performing arts. The empire provided extensive patronage to classical dance forms such as

Bharatanatyam, Kuchipudi, and Odissi. Court musicians and dancers enjoyed high status, and their performances were integral to royal ceremonies and public festivals. The performances celebrated the diverse cultural traditions of the empire, serving as a unifying force that brought together people from various backgrounds and languages. They embodied the spirit of inclusivity and cultural amalgamation. The Vijayanagara period witnessed the creation of numerous compositions in both music and dance. These compositions continue to form a vital part of the classical repertoire, reflecting the enduring legacy of Vijayanagara's contribution to the performing arts.

6) Urban Planning and Fortifications:

While not as prominently recognized as other art forms, the Vijayanagara Empire's architectural achievements extended to urban planning and fortifications. The capital city of Vijayanagara, Hampi, exemplified well-planned streets, markets, and water supply systems. This urban planning not only facilitated daily life but also showcased the empire's administrative acumen. The empire fortified its cities with walls, watchtowers, and military structures, reflecting its military prowess and its commitment to protecting its territories. These fortifications served as both practical defensive measures and statements of power.

2.2.2 Architecture in Vijaynagar Empire:

Architecture in the Vijayanagara Empire, which thrived in South India from the 14th to the 17th century, is renowned for its grandeur, innovation, and a unique fusion of indigenous Dravidian styles with elements of Islamic architecture. The empire's architectural achievements have left an indelible mark on the cultural heritage of India.

A) Emergence of Architecture During Vijaynagar Empire :

The Vijayanagara Empire, which thrived in South India from the 14th to the 17th century, witnessed the emergence of a distinct architectural style that combined elements of indigenous Indian architecture with Dravidian, Islamic, and Indo-Saracenic influences. The emergence of architecture during the Vijayanagara Empire is characterized by several significant developments:

1) Temples as Centerpieces:

Temples played a central role in the architectural landscape of the Vijayanagara Empire. These temples were monumental and often served as the focal point of urban planning, with large courtyards, impressive gopurams (temple towers), and intricately carved pillars.

2) Dravidian Architectural Style:

The Vijayanagara architecture predominantly followed the Dravidian architectural style, characterized by its pyramidal temple towers, intricate sculptures, and use of richly colored materials. The construction of massive and ornate gopurams was a hallmark of this style.

3) **Vitthala Temple Complex:**
The Vitthala Temple complex in Hampi is a prime example of the architectural grandeur of the Vijayanagara Empire. It features the iconic stone chariot and musical pillars, which are celebrated for their architectural & sculptural excellence.

4) **Monuments and Palaces:**
The empire constructed monumental structures, including palaces, audience halls, and other royal edifices. The Lotus Mahal, with its Indo-Islamic architectural influence, and the Queen's Bath are examples of the secular architecture of the period.

5) **Military Architecture:**
The empire built impressive fortifications, such as the Rayagad and the Chandragiri Fort, which were strategically designed for defense. These forts featured robust walls and bastions.

6) **Urban Planning:**
The capital city, Vijayanagara (Hampi), was meticulously planned and featured broad avenues, marketplaces, and an efficient drainage system. The sacred center of the city housed numerous temples, reflecting the spiritual and cultural significance of the empire.

7) **Innovative Use of Stone:**
The Vijayanagara architects made innovative use of stone in construction, including the use of large stone blocks, finely sculpted pillars, and intricately carved walls. The architectural marvels of the empire showcased the skill and creativity of its artisans.

8) **Bronze Sculptures:**
The empire was known for producing exquisite bronze sculptures, particularly of deities. These sculptures featured intricate details and were celebrated for their artistic and religious significance.

9) **Mural Paintings:**
The Vijayanagara period saw the creation of mural paintings within temple complexes. These paintings, often found on the ceilings of temple corridors, depicted various themes, including mythological stories and daily life.

10) **Cultural Patronage:**
The Vijayanagara rulers were great patrons of the arts, supporting poets, scholars, musicians, and dancers. The empire was a cultural hub, fostering the growth of literature and performing arts.

11) **Water Management:**
The empire was known for its water management systems, including tanks and reservoirs, which served both agricultural and urban needs. The complex aqueducts and water channels are a testament to their engineering expertise.

12) Legacy:

The architectural and artistic legacy of the Vijayanagara Empire has left an enduring mark on South Indian art and culture. Many of the architectural and artistic elements developed during this period continued to influence later dynasties and are celebrated as a part of India's rich cultural heritage.

B) Development of Architecture during Vijaynagar Empire:

During the Vijayanagara Empire, which thrived in South India from the 14th to the 17th century, architecture was one of the most significant and enduring art forms. The empire's architectural achievements left an indelible mark on the cultural heritage of India. Here are the major features and art forms within architecture during the Vijayanagara Empire:

1) Dravidian Architectural Style:

The Vijayanagara Empire predominantly followed the Dravidian architectural style, characterized by certain key elements. This style originated in Southern India and was known for its grandeur, ornate decoration, and intricate carvings.

2) Gopurams (Pyramidal Gateway Towers):

Gopurams are towering entrance gateways leading into temple complexes. They are a hallmark of Dravidian architecture and serve as iconic features of South Indian temples. These structures were often adorned with intricate sculptures and elaborate relief work depicting various deities and mythological scenes.

3) Mandapas (Halls):

Mandapas are large, pillared halls within temple complexes. They were designed to accommodate large congregations of devotees during religious ceremonies and festivals. The pillars in these mandapas were intricately carved with figures of deities, celestial beings, and mythological scenes. The thousand-pillared hall at the Ekambareswarar Temple in Kanchipuram is a notable example of this architectural feature.

4) Vimanas (Towers):

Vimanas are the towering structures that crown the sanctum sanctorum (garbhagriha) of a temple. They are often pyramid-shaped and adorned with intricate carvings. The vimanas of the Vijayanagara temples, such as the Virupaksha Temple and the Vittala Temple in Hampi, are noteworthy for their architectural elegance and artistic detailing.

5) Compound Walls:

Temple complexes in the Vijayanagara Empire were often enclosed by high compound walls, providing a sense of sanctity and privacy to the sacred space within. These walls were typically plain but sometimes featured decorative elements like relief sculptures or niches.

6) **Kalyana Mandapas (Marriage Halls):**

Some temples in the Vijayanagara Empire featured specialized halls known as Kalyana Mandapas. These were used for conducting marriage ceremonies of deities during festive occasions. The pillars and walls of these halls were adorned with intricate carvings depicting scenes from Hindu mythology.

7) **Aqueducts and Water Structures:**

The Vijayanagara Empire paid attention to water management and often incorporated aqueducts, tanks, and water channels within temple complexes. These structures were not only functional but also served aesthetic and architectural purposes.

8) **Stellate Plans:**

Some Vijayanagara temples featured stellate (star-shaped) plans, characterized by multiple projections or arms radiating out from a central core. This architectural feature added complexity and visual interest to the temple layouts.

9) **Monolithic Structures:**

The Vijayanagara Empire was known for the creation of monolithic structures, where entire temples or sculptures were carved from single blocks of stone. One of the most famous examples is the monolithic statue of Lord Ganesha in Hampi.

10) **Incorporation of Islamic Elements:**

While primarily rooted in Dravidian architecture, the Vijayanagara style also incorporated certain Islamic architectural elements, showcasing a unique synthesis of influences.

B) **Importance of Vijaynagar Empire in Architecture:**

The Vijayanagara Empire, which thrived in South India from the 14th to the 17th century, holds immense importance in the realm of architecture. The architectural legacy of the Vijayanagara Empire is a testament to the grandeur, innovation, and artistic brilliance of the period. It left an indelible mark on the cultural heritage of India and continues to be celebrated for its monumental structures, intricate carvings, and unique architectural style. Here, we will explore the significance of the Vijayanagara Empire in the field of architecture:

1) **Synthesis of Architectural Styles:**

One of the most remarkable aspects of Vijayanagara architecture is its synthesis of various architectural styles. It blended indigenous Dravidian architectural elements with influences from Islamic and other regional styles, resulting in a unique architectural tradition. This fusion of diverse influences created a distinctive architectural identity that set the Vijayanagara Empire apart.

2) **Dravidian Architectural Excellence:**

The Vijayanagara Empire was a torchbearer of Dravidian architecture. Dravidian architecture, which originated in South India, is characterized by grand temple complexes, towering gopurams (pyramidal entrance towers), ornate pillars, and intricate sculptures. The empire not only embraced these elements but also elevated them to new heights. The monumental temples of Vijayanagara, such as the Virupaksha Temple in Hampi, showcase the grandeur and intricacy of Dravidian architecture.

3) **Iconic Temple Architecture:**
The Vijayanagara Empire's contribution to temple architecture is particularly noteworthy. The empire was a great patron of temple construction, and its architects designed and built colossal temples dedicated to various deities. These temples are known for their monumental gopurams, intricately carved pillars, and stunning vimanas (towering structures over the sanctum sanctorum). The iconic Virupaksha Temple and the Vittala Temple in Hampi are enduring examples of this architectural excellence.

4) **Ornate Sculptures and Relief Work:**
The Vijayanagara Empire's architectural marvels were adorned with exquisite sculptures and intricate relief work. Skilled sculptors created detailed depictions of deities, mythological figures, and celestial beings. These artistic elements not only enhanced the aesthetic beauty of the structures but also served as a means of storytelling and religious symbolism.

5) **Innovative Features:**
Vijayanagara architecture introduced several innovative features. The empire's architects designed elaborately carved pillared halls (mandapas) within temple complexes, enabling large congregations during religious ceremonies. The raya-mandapa, a community hall for gatherings and performances, was another architectural innovation of the period.

6) **Cultural Integration:**
The Vijayanagara Empire's architectural achievements were a reflection of its commitment to cultural integration. The empire was home to people from various backgrounds, languages, and faiths. Its architecture served as a unifying force, bringing together diverse cultural traditions and fostering an inclusive society.

7) **Enduring Legacy:**
The architectural legacy of the Vijayanagara Empire continues to captivate and inspire generations of art enthusiasts, architects, and scholars. The temples, gopurams, and monolithic sculptures created during this period stand as a testament to the empire's cultural richness and creative genius.

8) **Influence on Subsequent Architectural Traditions:**
The architectural innovations of the Vijayanagara Empire had a profound and lasting impact on subsequent South Indian temple architecture. The principles and styles developed during this period continue to influence architectural practices and temple construction in the region. The fusion of indigenous and external influences

that characterized Vijayanagara architecture is a testament to the empire's adaptability and open-mindedness.

2.3 Maratha:

The Marathas, a warrior and agrarian community from western India, rose to prominence in the 17th century under the leadership of Chhatrapati Shivaji Maharaj. They established the Maratha Empire, which spanned a vast territory in India. Known for their military prowess, the Marathas successfully challenged the Mughal Empire's dominance, carving out a significant regional power. However, the empire later faced internal conflicts and external pressures, notably from the British East India Company, leading to its decline. The Marathas left a lasting legacy in Indian history, with their contributions in administration, culture, and warfare shaping the socio-political landscape of India.

2.3.1 Arts in Maratha Empire:

The Maratha Empire, which existed from the late 17th century to the early 19th century in the Indian subcontinent, had a rich and diverse cultural heritage. Arts in the Maratha Empire encompassed a wide range of creative expressions, including architecture, painting, music, dance, and literature.

A) Emergence of Arts During Maratha Empire :

The Maratha Empire, which emerged in the 17th century in India and reached its zenith in the 18th century, witnessed the flourishing of various art forms and cultural expressions. The emergence of arts during the Maratha Empire is characterized by several key developments:

1) Painting:

Maratha painting primarily developed in the form of miniatures and murals. Maratha rulers and nobility were patrons of the arts, and they commissioned artists to create intricate and detailed paintings that often depicted court scenes, portraits of rulers, and mythological themes. These paintings displayed a blend of indigenous Indian artistic traditions and Persian influences.

2) Sculpture:

Maratha sculptors created intricate stone carvings and sculptures, especially in temple architecture. The Maratha temples in Maharashtra are known for their finely crafted sculptures of deities, mythological figures, and ornate ornamentation.

3) Temple Architecture:

The Marathas contributed to the construction and renovation of temples across Maharashtra. These temples typically followed the Deccan architectural style, which combined elements of Dravidian and Indo-Aryan styles. The architecture featured intricately carved pillars, mandapas, and gopurams (temple towers).

4) **Music and Dance:**
The Maratha Empire was a patron of classical music and dance. The Marathi classical musical tradition developed during this period, which includes various forms of classical music and musical instruments. The Lavani dance form also gained prominence during the Maratha rule.

5) **Literature:**
Marathi literature flourished during the Maratha Empire. Renowned Marathi poets and writers like Sant Eknath, Tukaram, and Ramdas contributed significantly to Marathi literature. The literature of this period included devotional poetry, mythological narratives, and social and moralistic literature.

6) **Textiles and Handicrafts:**
The Marathas were known for their patronage of textile and handicraft industries. Intricate handwoven textiles, such as Paithani and Himroo, became popular. Various handicrafts, including Bidriware and Kolhapuri chappals, gained recognition during this era.

7) **Mural Paintings:**
Some Maratha forts, such as the Raigad Fort, featured mural paintings on their walls. These paintings often depicted scenes from Maratha history, including heroic tales and events related to the Maratha rulers.

8) **Folk Arts:**
Maratha regions saw the continuation and preservation of traditional folk arts and crafts. The Warli paintings of Maharashtra and the Gond art of Madhya Pradesh are examples of indigenous folk art that continued to thrive during this period.

9) **Architecture:**
While not as renowned for its architecture as some earlier dynasties, the Maratha Empire did contribute to the construction and renovation of forts and palaces. Many of these structures featured architectural elements influenced by the prevailing styles of the time.

10) **Cultural Fusion:**
The Maratha Empire, with its expansive territorial influence, facilitated cultural exchanges and interactions between different regions. This led to a fusion of artistic and cultural elements, resulting in a diverse and rich cultural tapestry.

B) Development of Art forms During Maratha Empire :

Following are the major art forms that thrived during the Maratha Empire.

1) **Architecture:**
The Maratha Empire was known for its architectural achievements, which included the construction of forts, palaces, temples, and urban planning.

2) **Fortifications:**
The Marathas built strategically located and well-fortified forts, such as Raigad Fort and Pratapgad Fort. These forts were not only military strongholds but also centers

of administration. Maratha rulers were patrons of temple construction. Their temples often incorporated elements of indigenous styles, showcasing intricate stonework and ornate pillars. The Marathas constructed opulent palaces, with Shaniwar Wada in Pune being a notable example. These palaces reflected their refined tastes and architectural grandeur. The Marathas emphasized well-planned cities and town layouts with wide streets, markets, and efficient water supply systems. These urban planning initiatives improved the quality of life and contributed to the overall development of the empire.

3) Painting:

The Maratha Empire nurtured a vibrant tradition of painting, primarily focusing on miniature paintings that depicted a range of subjects. Maratha miniature paintings captured scenes from epics, mythological narratives, and royal court life. They were characterized by intricate detailing, vibrant colors, and an emphasis on conveying expressions and emotions. Maratha rulers were enthusiastic patrons of the arts, including painting. Their support allowed Maratha artists to thrive and create enduring works of art. Maratha painting contributed to India's cultural landscape and had a lasting impact on regional painting styles. It played a crucial role in preserving and conveying stories from Hindu mythology and history.

4) Music and Dance:

Music and dance were integral to Maratha culture, featuring classical and folk art forms that served both religious and entertainment purposes. The Marathas had a strong tradition of Hindustani classical music, with the courts of Maratha rulers being known for their support of musicians and composers. This patronage significantly contributed to the development of classical music in India. Maratha dance forms, such as Lavani and Tamasha, were popular in the region. Lavani was a traditional Maharashtrian dance known for its vibrant and rhythmic movements, while Tamasha was a folk dance-drama form featuring themes of love and social issues.Religious Music and Dance: Maratha temples and festivals often featured devotional music and dance performances as a form of worship and cultural expression. These performances celebrated the rich cultural and spiritual heritage of the Marathas.

5) Literature:

Maratha literature encompassed a wide range of writings in Marathi, Sanskrit, and other regional languages. It included poetry, prose, historical chronicles, and religious texts. The Maratha Empire played a pivotal role in the development of Marathi literature. Renowned poets and scholars, such as Tukaram and Ramdas, made significant contributions by creating devotional poetry and philosophical works. Sanskrit continued to be a language of literary expression during the Maratha Empire, with scholars composing works that reflected the cultural and spiritual ethos of the time. The Marathas had a strong tradition of documenting their history and achievements. Historical chronicles and biographies were written to preserve the legacy of Maratha rulers, particularly Shivaji. The empire witnessed the composition of religious texts and philosophical treatises that explored spiritual themes and ethical principles.

6) Folk Arts and Crafts:

The Maratha Empire celebrated various folk arts and crafts, including pottery, handloom textiles, and traditional crafts.These art forms often had a utilitarian aspect, with artisans producing items for everyday use, such as pottery, textiles, and jewelry. Folk traditions, such as Warli painting, thrived and depicted scenes from rural life and mythology, adding to the cultural richness of the region.

C) Importance of Maratha Empire in Arts:

The Maratha Empire, which existed from the late 17th century to the early 19th century, played a significant role in the development and promotion of arts in India.

1) Patronage of Indigenous Art Forms:

The Maratha Empire was a fervent supporter of traditional Indian art forms such as classical music, dance, painting, and literature. The rulers recognized the cultural significance of these forms and actively promoted their preservation and development.

2) Nurturing Classical Music:

Maratha rulers, including Shivaji and subsequent emperors, were ardent patrons of classical music, particularly Hindustani classical music. The Maratha courts became hubs of musical excellence, attracting and nurturing renowned musicians, composers, and performers.This patronage not only elevated the status of classical music but also contributed to the evolution and enrichment of the art form. It provided a platform for musicians to refine their skills and create enduring compositions.

3) Celebration of Dance Forms:

The Maratha Empire embraced traditional dance forms like Lavani and Tamasha. These vibrant and expressive dance forms originated in Maharashtra and became integral to the cultural landscape.Maratha rulers provided platforms for artists to showcase their talents, allowing these dance forms to flourish. This celebration of dance not only provided entertainment but also served as a means of cultural expression.

4) Promotion of Painting:

Maratha painting, influenced by Mughal and Rajput styles but with distinct characteristics, experienced a significant renaissance. The empire's rulers recognized the importance of visual arts as a medium for storytelling and cultural expression.Maratha miniature paintings depicted a wide range of subjects, including mythological narratives and scenes from court life. These paintings not only served as aesthetic creations but also played a vital role in preserving and disseminating cultural narratives.

5) **Encouragement of Literature:**

Maratha rulers fostered a flourishing literary tradition. They supported the development of Marathi literature, Sanskrit compositions, and other regional languages. This patronage gave rise to a diverse body of literary works.Prominent poets and scholars, such as Tukaram and Ramdas, made significant contributions to Marathi literature, producing devotional poetry and philosophical treatises. Historical chronicles and religious texts were also written to preserve the legacy and cultural heritage of the Maratha Empire.

6) **Cultural Legacy and Influence:**

The artistic legacy of the Maratha Empire continues to be celebrated and admired in contemporary India. Many of the art forms that thrived during this period have left a lasting impact on the cultural heritage of the Indian subcontinent. The Marathas' patronage of the arts, their regional influences, and their unique artistic expressions have contributed to a rich and diverse cultural tapestry that endures to this day.

2.3.2 Architecture in Maratha Empire:

Architecture during the Maratha Empire was characterized by a blend of indigenous styles with regional influences, reflecting the diverse cultural and historical context of the time. The Maratha Empire's architectural achievements, particularly in the construction of forts, palaces, temples, and urban planning, are significant and have left a lasting impact.

A) Emergence of Architecture During Maratha Empire :

The Maratha Empire, which rose to prominence in the 17th century and reached its zenith in the 18th century, made significant contributions to the field of architecture. The emergence of architecture during the Maratha Empire is marked by the development of unique regional architectural styles, the construction of forts, palaces, temples, and the preservation of indigenous architectural traditions. Here are the key features of architecture during the Maratha Empire:

1) **Maratha Forts:**

The Marathas were known for their strategic fortifications. They constructed and improved numerous forts across their dominions. These forts were characterized by strong fortifications, bastions, and gateways. The Raigad Fort, under the rule of Chhatrapati Shivaji, is an iconic example of Maratha fort architecture. The Marathas combined their military and architectural prowess to create formidable defensive structures.

2) Military Architecture:

The Marathas developed distinctive military architectural techniques to withstand enemy attacks. They employed natural topography to their advantage and designed forts with layered defenses, including moats, drawbridges, and multiple gateways. The architecture of these forts was designed to withstand prolonged sieges.

3) Palaces and Residences:

The Marathas constructed palaces for their rulers and nobility. The Shaniwar Wada in Pune, a palace fort, is a well-known example. These palaces were characterized by grand courtyards, intricate woodwork, and spacious living quarters. Maratha palace architecture often combined elements of Mughal and regional architectural styles.

4) Temple Architecture:

The Marathas made significant contributions to temple architecture. They constructed and renovated Hindu temples in the Deccan architectural style. Maratha temples often featured ornate entrance gates, mandapas (pillared halls), and intricately carved stone sculptures of deities. The Kashi Vishveshwar Temple in Varanasi is an example of Maratha-style temple architecture.

5) Mughal Influence:

The Marathas, particularly during the Peshwa rule, were influenced by Mughal architecture. The Peshwa rulers adopted elements of Mughal architectural design in their buildings. The Shaniwar Wada, for instance, exhibits a fusion of Maratha and Mughal architectural elements.

6) Courtyards and Gardens:

Maratha architecture emphasized the use of courtyards and gardens within palace complexes. These open spaces were designed for relaxation, social gatherings, and ceremonial functions. The Shaniwar Wada, for example, featured a large courtyard at its center.

7) Architectural Ornamentation:

Maratha architecture incorporated intricate carvings, including floral motifs, geometric designs, and depictions of deities and mythological scenes. The Ajanta Caves, which were renovated during the Maratha rule, showcase this artistic and architectural fusion.

8) Influence on Later Dynasties:

The architectural innovations of the Maratha Empire had a lasting impact on later dynasties in the Deccan, including the Gaekwads of Baroda and the Scindias of Gwalior. The architectural styles developed during the Maratha period continued to influence the region's subsequent architectural endeavors.

9) Cultural and Religious Tolerance:

Maratha architecture reflected the empire's cultural and religious diversity. Buildings were constructed for various religious communities, showcasing the empire's policy of religious tolerance and cultural inclusivity.

B) Development of Architecture During Maratha Empire:

During the Maratha Empire, which existed from the late 17th century to the early 19th century, architecture was a significant art form that flourished. The Maratha Empire's architectural achievements were characterized by a blend of indigenous styles with influences from various regions. Here are the major art forms within architecture during the Maratha Empire:

1) Forts:

The Marathas were renowned for their strong and strategically positioned forts. These forts served both defensive and administrative purposes. They were constructed with robust defensive features, including walls, bastions, and watchtowers.

Notable examples include Raigad Fort, Pratapgad Fort, Sinhagad Fort, and Janjira Fort. Each of these forts demonstrated unique architectural characteristics and played a crucial role in the empire's defense.

2) Palaces:

The Maratha rulers constructed opulent palaces, reflecting their refined tastes and architectural grandeur. Palaces served as seats of power and cultural centers. The Shaniwar Wada in Pune stands as a prominent example of Maratha palace architecture.

3) Temples:

The Maratha Empire was a patron of temple construction. The temples built during this period often incorporated elements of indigenous architectural styles. They featured intricate stonework, ornate pillars, and elaborately carved sculptures depicting various deities.

4) Urban Planning:

The Marathas were known for their well-planned cities and town layouts. They emphasized wide streets, markets, and efficient water supply systems. This urban planning initiative improved the quality of life and contributed to the overall development of the empire.

5) Cultural Integration:

Maratha architecture demonstrated a cultural fusion of indigenous styles with influences from the Deccan region and other parts of India. This integration showcased the empire's adaptability and its ability to harmonize diverse architectural traditions.

6) **Water Structures:**
Maratha architecture also paid attention to water management. It featured aqueducts, tanks, and water channels within cities and towns. These structures served functional as well as aesthetic and architectural purposes.

D) **Importance of Maratha Empire in Architecture:**
The Maratha Empire, which thrived from the late 17th century to the early 19th century, holds significant importance in the field of architecture for several reasons:

1) **Synthesis of Architectural Styles:**
The Maratha Empire was situated in a region with diverse cultural and architectural influences. It successfully synthesized indigenous styles with elements from the Deccan, Mughal, and other regional architectural traditions. This fusion created a distinctive architectural identity that reflected the empire's cultural diversity.

2) **Fortification Expertise:**
The Marathas were known for their military prowess, and their forts stand as architectural marvels. These forts were strategically constructed on elevated positions, showcasing advanced knowledge of defensive architecture. Notable forts like Raigad and Pratapgad are enduring examples of Maratha fortification expertise.

3) **Opulent Palaces:**
Maratha rulers were patrons of opulent palace architecture. Palaces like the Shaniwar Wada in Pune were not only administrative centers but also cultural hubs. They reflected the refined tastes and architectural grandeur of the Maratha rulers.

4) **Temple Patronage:**
The Marathas were patrons of temple construction, contributing significantly to regional temple architecture. These temples incorporated elements of indigenous styles, with intricate stonework, ornate pillars, and detailed sculptures. They played a crucial role in preserving and promoting Hindu religious and cultural traditions.

5) **Urban Planning Initiatives:**
The Marathas emphasized well-planned cities and town layouts, featuring wide streets, markets, and efficient water supply systems. This urban planning initiative not only enhanced the quality of life for residents but also demonstrated the empire's commitment to organized urban development.

6) **Cultural Integration:**
Maratha architecture reflected a cultural fusion of indigenous styles with influences from various regions of India. This integration showcased the empire's adaptability and its ability to harmonize diverse architectural traditions. It served as a unifying force in a region characterized by cultural heterogeneity.

7) **Water Management Systems:**
Maratha architecture paid attention to water management. It featured aqueducts, tanks, and water channels within cities and towns. These structures served both

functional and aesthetic purposes, reflecting the empire's holistic approach to urban planning.

8) **Legacy and Influence:**
The architectural legacy of the Maratha Empire continues to be celebrated and admired. Many of the forts, palaces, and temples constructed during this period have stood the test of time and continue to be important cultural and historical landmarks.

♦♦♦

Review Questions

Q.1. Answer the Following Questions:

1) Discuss about the Emergence and Development of Art during Bahamani Sultanate
2) Explain Importance of Art in Bahamani Sultanate.
3) Write about the Emergence and Development of Architecture during Bahamani Sultanate.
4) Explain the Importance of Architecture in Bahamani Sultanate.
5) Explain Emergence and Development of Art during Vijaynagar.
6) State the Importance of Art in Vijaynagar Empire.
7) Explain Emergence and Development of Architecture during Vijaynagar.
8) Discuss the Importance of Architecture in Vijaynagar Empire.
9) Explain Emergence and Development of Art during Maratha Empire.
10) State the Importance of Art in Maratha Empire.
11) Explain Emergence and Development of Architecture during Maratha Empire.
12) Discuss the Importance of Architecture in Maratha Empire.

Q.2. Write Short Notes on:

1) Art in Bahamani.
2) Architecture in Bahamani.
3) Art in Vijaynagar.
4) Architecture in Vijaynagar.
5) Art in Maratha.
6) Architecture in Maratha.

♦♦♦

UNIT 3

Development of Sur and Mughal Art & Architecture

Introduction:

The development of Sur and Mughal art and architecture in the Indian subcontinent represents a captivating journey spanning centuries, characterized by a fusion of indigenous artistic traditions with external influences. The Sur dynasty (c. 1540-1556) ushered in a distinctive artistic era marked by a syncretic blend of Persian and Indian elements. Sur architecture, exemplified by Sher Shah Suri's Grand Trunk Road and the Rohtas Fort, showcased innovative techniques in road construction and fortification. However, the Mughal Empire (c. 1526-1857) brought forth a golden age of art and architecture that left an indelible mark on the subcontinent's cultural landscape. The Mughals, particularly under the reign of Akbar, Jahangir, Shah Jahan, and Aurangzeb, nurtured a flourishing artistic environment characterized by the splendid Mughal Gardens, intricate miniature paintings, and grand architectural wonders like the Taj Mahal, the Red Fort, and the Jama Masjid. These structures embodied the Mughal penchant for opulence, symmetry, and the fusion of Persian and Indian design elements. Furthermore, the Mughals greatly patronized the arts, leading to the emergence of renowned artists such as Abul Hasan, Bishandas, and Govardhan. The Mughal artistic legacy also included illuminated manuscripts like the Akbarnama, exquisite textiles, and the development of regional artistic schools. The amalgamation of diverse cultural influences during this period has left an enduring impact, shaping the artistic and architectural heritage of the Indian subcontinent for generations to come.

3.1 Qila-Kunha-Masjid:

The Qila-Kunha-Masjid, also known as the Quila Kunha Mosque, is a historical mosque located in Delhi, India. It holds significant historical and architectural importance in the region.

3.1.1 Aspects of Qila-Kunha-Masjid:

Here are key points about the Qila-Kunha-Masjid:

1) **Historical Context**:
   The Qila-Kunha-Masjid is situated within the premises of the historic Purana Qila (Old Fort) complex in Delhi. The construction of the Purana Qila dates back to the 16th century during the reign of the Mughal emperor Humayun.
2) **Mughal Architecture**:
   This mosque is a fine example of Mughal architecture, characterized by its distinct features such as red sandstone construction, domes, and intricate decorative elements. It reflects the architectural style prevalent during the Mughal period in India.
3) **Construction Date**:
   The mosque was built in the mid-16th century during the reign of the Mughal emperor Sher Shah Suri (reigned 1540-1545). Sher Shah Suri, though not a Mughal, made significant contributions to the architectural landscape of North India.
4) **Sher Shah Suri's Reign**:
   Sher Shah Suri was known for his administrative and military prowess. During his reign, he undertook various construction projects, including roads, forts, and mosques, to improve the infrastructure of his empire. The Qila-Kunha-Masjid is one such architectural legacy.
5) **Purpose**:
   The primary purpose of the Qila-Kunha-Masjid was to serve as a place of worship for the residents and visitors to the Purana Qila complex. Mosques during this era not only held religious significance but also served as centers for community gatherings and social interactions.
6) **Architecture and Design**:
   The mosque features a simple yet elegant design. It is built using red sandstone, which was a common building material during the Mughal and Suri periods. The mosque's main prayer hall is crowned with three domes, one larger central dome flanked by two smaller ones. The use of domes is a characteristic feature of Mughal and Indo-Islamic architecture.
7) **Inscriptions**:
   The mosque bears inscriptions in Arabic and Persian calligraphy, which include verses from the Quran and other religious texts. These inscriptions not only serve a decorative purpose but also convey religious messages to the worshippers.

8) **Courtyard**:
Like many other mosques of the period, the Qila-Kunha-Masjid has a spacious courtyard. The courtyard provides an open area for worshippers to gather, especially during congregational prayers on Fridays and during religious festivals.

9) **Conservation and Restoration**:
Over the centuries, the mosque has undergone several rounds of restoration and conservation efforts to preserve its historical and architectural significance. Government authorities and heritage organizations have worked to maintain the structure and its surroundings.

10) **Tourist Attraction**:
Today, the Qila-Kunha-Masjid is a popular tourist attraction within the Purana Qila complex. Visitors can explore the mosque's architecture, historical inscriptions, and the tranquil atmosphere that surrounds it. It serves as a reminder of the rich architectural heritage of Delhi and the contributions of rulers like Sher Shah Suri to the city's history.

3.1.2 Historical Importance of Qila-Kunha-Masjid:

Historical Importance of Qila-Kunha-Masjid explained with following points:

1) **Mughal Architectural Heritage:**
Qila-i-Kuhna Mosque, situated within the premises of the Purana Qila (Old Fort) in Delhi, stands as a significant example of Mughal architectural prowess and cultural legacy.

2) **Sher Shah's Mosque:**
Initially constructed by Sher Shah Suri, it served as a mosque within the Sher Mandal complex, showcasing the transition from the Sur dynasty to the Mughal era.

3) **Blend of Architectural Styles:**
The mosque embodies a fusion of diverse architectural styles, combining elements of Afghan and Mughal architecture, showcasing the cultural amalgamation during that period.

4) **Intricate Designs:**
The mosque exhibits intricate designs, including decorative carvings, inscriptions in Persian, and ornate calligraphy, reflecting the artistic brilliance of Mughal craftsmanship.

5) **Historical Significance:**
The mosque's historical importance lies in its association with prominent historical figures like Sher Shah Suri and Humayun, reflecting the political transitions and dynastic changes during that period.

6) **Religious Significance:**
As a place of worship, the mosque signifies the religious and cultural heritage of the Mughal era, serving as a symbol of faith and spirituality.

7) **Architectural Conservation:**

Its preservation and restoration efforts by archaeological departments and conservationists highlight its significance as a cultural heritage site, contributing to the understanding of Mughal architecture.

8) **Tourist Attraction:**

The mosque, located within the Old Fort complex, attracts tourists, history enthusiasts, and scholars interested in Mughal history, architecture, and cultural heritage.

9) **Cultural Symbolism:**

The mosque stands as a cultural symbol, representing the legacy of the Mughal Empire and its architectural contributions to India's rich heritage.

10) **Historical Context:**

Qila-i-Kuhna Mosque's location within the Old Fort contextualizes its historical significance, linking it to the broader historical narrative of Delhi and its significance in the annals of Indian history.

3.2 Tombs of Hasan Sur and Sher Shah:

The tombs of Hasan Suri and Sher Shah Suri, located in Sasaram, Bihar, India, are two remarkable architectural and historical landmarks that bear witness to the legacy of the Suri dynasty. Hasan Suri's tomb, the grandfather of Sher Shah Suri, is a testament to the dynasty's early influence, featuring a relatively simple yet elegant red sandstone structure with inscriptions in Arabic and Persian script. In contrast, Sher Shah Suri's tomb, one of the most distinguished examples of Indo-Islamic architecture, is a grand mausoleum that stands as a tribute to Sher Shah's significant contributions to the administration and infrastructure of North India during his reign in the mid-16th century. This ornate tomb boasts a striking octagonal design, intricate carving, a massive central dome, and beautifully landscaped gardens, reflecting the zenith of Mughal architectural sophistication. Together, these tombs encapsulate the historical and cultural richness of the Suri dynasty, inviting visitors to explore the dynastic history and architectural excellence of this era.

3.2.1 Tombs of Hasan Sur:

The tomb of Hasan Suri, also known as Hasan Khan Suri's Tomb, is a historical monument located in Sasaram, Bihar, India. While it may not be as renowned as some other tombs in India, it holds significance as a representation of the early Suri dynasty's architectural style and historical legacy. Here are key points about Hasan Suri's Tomb:

1) **Historical Context**:

Hasan Suri was the grandfather of Sher Shah Suri, a prominent ruler who briefly established the Suri dynasty in Northern India during the mid-16th century. Hasan Suri's tomb is a testament to the family's growing prominence during this period.

2) **Location**:
The tomb is situated in Sasaram, a town in Bihar, and is relatively close to the more famous Sher Shah Suri's Tomb. The proximity of these two tombs underscores their historical connection and the Suri dynasty's presence in the region.

3) **Architecture Style**:
Hasan Suri's Tomb reflects the architectural style prevalent during the early years of the Suri dynasty. It features a relatively simple design compared to later Mughal tombs. The primary building material used is red sandstone, a common choice for Indo-Islamic architecture.

4) **Structure**:
The tomb is constructed in the form of a square building topped with a single dome. The dome is a significant feature of Indo-Islamic architecture and serves as a symbol of the celestial dome of heaven.

5) **Decorative Elements**:
Despite its simplicity, the tomb does feature some decorative elements. The dome is adorned with traditional Islamic geometric and floral patterns, showcasing the artistic influences of the era.

6) **Inscriptions**:
Like many historical monuments, Hasan Suri's Tomb bears inscriptions in Arabic and Persian script. These inscriptions provide valuable historical information about Hasan Suri's lineage and the period in which the tomb was constructed. They serve as an important resource for historians and researchers.

7) **Purpose**:
The primary purpose of Hasan Suri's tomb was to serve as a final resting place for him. However, it also acted as a symbol of the family's status and influence in the region during the early years of the Suri dynasty.

8) **Historical Significance**:
While Hasan Suri's reign and contributions may not be as extensively documented or celebrated as those of his grandson Sher Shah Suri, his tomb remains an important historical marker. It helps us understand the early rise of the Suri dynasty and its role in shaping the history of Northern India.

9) **Conservation Efforts**:
Over the years, there have been efforts to conserve and maintain Hasan Suri's Tomb. Government authorities and heritage organizations have worked to ensure the preservation of this historical monument and its inscriptions.

10) **Tourist Attraction**:
While not as well-known as some other historical sites in India, Hasan Suri's Tomb does attract tourists and history enthusiasts. Visitors can explore the architecture, inscriptions, and the historical significance of this lesser-known gem within the rich tapestry of India's historical and architectural heritage.

3.2.2 Tombs of Sher Shah:

Sher Shah Suri's Tomb, located in Sasaram, Bihar, India, is a remarkable architectural and historical masterpiece that pays homage to the legacy of Sher Shah Suri, a pivotal figure in Indian history during the mid-16th century. Here are key points about Sher Shah Suri's Tomb:

1) **Historical Background**:
   Sher Shah Suri, also known as Sher Khan, was a formidable ruler who founded the Suri dynasty in Northern India after defeating the Mughal Emperor Humayun in 1540. His reign brought significant administrative and infrastructural changes to the region.

2) **Tomb Location**:
   The tomb of Sher Shah Suri is situated in Sasaram, Bihar, which was the center of his power during his rule. Sasaram was strategically important due to its location on the Grand Trunk Road, a major trade and transportation route in India.

3) **Architectural Style**:
   Sher Shah Suri's Tomb is an exemplary piece of Indo-Islamic architecture. It is known for its distinct octagonal shape, which sets it apart from many other tombs of its time. The architectural style blends elements of Afghan and Indian architecture.

4) **Octagonal Design**:
   The tomb is built in the shape of an octagon, with each side measuring approximately 22 meters. This unique design is a significant departure from the traditional square or rectangular layouts commonly seen in Islamic architecture.

5) **Materials**:
   The primary building material used for the tomb is red sandstone, a prevalent choice for Indo-Islamic architecture. The sandstone gives the tomb its characteristic warm and rich color.

6) **Architectural Elements**:
   The tomb features a massive central dome that rises elegantly from a high platform. The dome is surrounded by smaller domed chhatris (pavilions), giving the tomb a symmetrical and aesthetically pleasing appearance.

7) **Decorative Features**:
   The exterior of the tomb is adorned with intricate decorative elements, including ornate calligraphy, geometric patterns, and delicate floral motifs. These carvings reflect the artistic excellence of the era.

8) **Inscriptions**:
   Like many historical monuments, Sher Shah Suri's Tomb bears inscriptions in Arabic and Persian script. These inscriptions provide information about the tomb's construction, Sher Shah Suri's reign, and the Suri dynasty's achievements.

9) **Gardens and Water Channels**:

The tomb is surrounded by well-maintained gardens and water channels, adding to its aesthetic appeal. The gardens are a common feature of Mughal and Indo-Islamic tombs, providing a tranquil environment for visitors.

10) **Historical Significance**:

Sher Shah Suri's Tomb holds immense historical significance as a tribute to his reign and contributions. His rule marked a period of effective administration, military reforms, and infrastructure development, including the construction of the Grand Trunk Road.

3.3 Akbar:

Akbar the Great, also known as Jalal-ud-din Muhammad Akbar, was one of the most prominent rulers in Indian history. He reigned from 1556 to 1605 and is often regarded as one of the greatest Mughal emperors. His reign marked a significant period of stability, cultural flourishing, and administrative innovation in the Indian subcontinent.

During Akbar's reign, art and architecture flourished, showcasing a unique blend of indigenous Indian styles with Persian, Central Asian, and European influences. Here are the features:

1) **Indo-Islamic Fusion:**

Akbar's era saw the fusion of Indian and Islamic artistic elements. This synthesis resulted in the development of a distinct style, visible in structures like Fatehpur Sikri's Buland Darwaza, combining Persian and Indian architectural motifs.

2) **Mughal Architecture:**

Akbar patronized grand architectural projects, including Agra Fort and the construction of the iconic Fatehpur Sikri complex, showcasing red sandstone structures, colossal gateways, expansive courtyards, and intricate carvings.

3) **Integration of Cultures:**

Akbar's court was a melting pot of diverse cultures, welcoming artists, architects, and intellectuals from various regions. This cultural integration influenced Mughal art and architecture, leading to a unique amalgamation of styles.

4) **Religious Tolerance:**

Akbar's policies of religious tolerance and inclusivity influenced artistic expression. This openness is evident in the architectural marvel of the Ibadat Khana at Fatehpur Sikri, symbolizing religious pluralism.

5) **Frescoes and Paintings:**

Akbar's era witnessed the development of Mughal painting, marked by intricate miniature paintings depicting court scenes, wildlife, and portraits. The Hamzanama and Akbarnama illustrate the artistic excellence of the time.

6) Use of Pietra Dura:

Akbar's reign saw the rise of pietra dura, an art form involving the inlay of semiprecious stones into marble surfaces. This technique adorned structures like the tomb of Itmad-ud-Daula in Agra.

7) Innovative Architecture:

Akbar's architects experimented with innovative structural designs, incorporating advanced engineering techniques in constructing massive domes, expansive courtyards, and intricate lattice work.

8) Cultural Syncretism:

Akbar's reign fostered cultural syncretism, encouraging cross-cultural exchanges that influenced art, music, literature, and architecture, leading to a rich artistic heritage.

9) Landscaped Gardens:

Akbar's fascination with nature led to the creation of exquisite gardens, such as the Charbagh at the Taj Mahal and the gardens at Fatehpur Sikri, blending Persian and Indian landscaping traditions.

10) Legacy of Monumental Structures:

The architectural legacy of Akbar's reign endures through monumental structures that stand as testaments to the era's artistic brilliance, cultural diversity, and architectural innovation.

3.3.1 The Tomb of Humayan:

The Tomb of Humayun, built in 1569-70, is a masterpiece of Mughal architecture located in Delhi, India. This historic monument is renowned for its bulbous dome, lush chahar bagh garden, and its influence on the design of the iconic Taj Mahal. Recognized as a UNESCO World Heritage Site, it stands as a testament to the rich cultural and architectural legacy of the Mughal Empire.

1) Historical Significance:

The Tomb of Humayun, located in Delhi, India, is an architectural marvel that holds immense historical significance. It is the final resting place of Emperor Humayun, the second Mughal emperor of India, and is considered one of the earliest examples of Mughal architecture.

2) Mughal Architecture:

The tomb is a prime example of Mughal architecture, which blends Persian, Central Asian, and Indian architectural styles. It is renowned for its use of red sandstone and white marble, intricate geometric patterns, and a distinctive bulbous dome that became a hallmark of Mughal architectural design.

3) **Construction Date**:

The construction of Humayun's Tomb was commissioned by Empress Bega Begum, also known as Haji Begum, the widow of Emperor Humayun, in 1569-70 AD. The tomb's completion marked a significant departure from the earlier architectural styles in the region.

4) **Architectural Innovation**:

The tomb was designed by the Persian architect Mirak Mirza Ghiyas, who introduced several architectural innovations, including the use of a high plinth and a symmetrical garden layout that would later influence the design of the Taj Mahal.

5) **Garden Complex**:

Humayun's Tomb is set within a vast garden complex known as a chahar bagh, a Persian-style garden divided into four quadrants by water channels and pathways. The meticulous planning of the garden is a reflection of the Persian concept of paradise gardens, symbolizing the earthly representation of paradise.

6) **Bulbous Dome**:

The tomb's most striking feature is its bulbous dome, which rises to a height of 42 meters (138 feet). This dome is considered a precursor to the more famous dome of the Taj Mahal and is a magnificent example of Indo-Islamic architecture.

7) **Influence on Taj Mahal**:

Humayun's Tomb is often cited as a precursor to the Taj Mahal, as it served as an architectural prototype for this iconic monument. The Taj Mahal, built by Emperor Shah Jahan, showcases a similar use of white marble, symmetry, and a central dome, all of which were inspired by Humayun's Tomb.

8) **Restoration and UNESCO World Heritage Site**:

Over the years, the tomb complex fell into disrepair. However, extensive restoration efforts were undertaken in the 20th century, and in 1993, it was designated as a UNESCO World Heritage Site. This recognition helped preserve and promote the historical and cultural significance of the monument.

9) **Integration of Persian and Indian Styles**:

Humayun's Tomb reflects the Mughal rulers' efforts to integrate Persian and Indian architectural elements. The use of Persian calligraphy and geometric patterns on the façade, combined with Indian elements like chhatris (domed pavilions), showcases this fusion of styles.

10) **Cultural Symbolism**:

The Tomb of Humayun stands not only as a testament to architectural brilliance but also as a cultural symbol. It represents the legacy of the Mughal Empire, its rich artistic traditions, and its contributions to the world of architecture. It continues to be a popular tourist destination and a source of pride for the people of India.

3.3.2 Agra Fort:

Agra Fort, a UNESCO World Heritage Site, is a historic fortress in Agra, India. Built during the Mughal era, it showcases a blend of Indian and Persian architectural styles with its distinctive red sandstone walls. Notable features include the Diwan-i-Am, Diwan-i-Khas, and the stunning Moti Masjid. Agra Fort played a significant role in Mughal history and offers a captivating glimpse into India's rich cultural heritage.

A) Architectural Features of Agra Fort:

Agra Fort, also known as the Red Fort of Agra, is a UNESCO World Heritage Site located in the city of Agra, Uttar Pradesh, India. It is a historic fortress that served as the main residence of the emperors of the Mughal Dynasty for several generations.

1) Architectural Layout:

The fort covers a vast area of about 94 acres, enclosed within massive red sandstone walls that stretch for approximately 2.5 kilometers, forming a nearly semi-circular enclosure. The fort's strategic location on the banks of the Yamuna River provides natural defenses on one side.

2) Entrances and Gates:

The fort features multiple entrances and gates, with the most prominent being the Amar Singh Gate and the Delhi Gate. The Amar Singh Gate served as the formal entrance to the fort, adorned with intricate embellishments and showcasing Mughal architectural finesse.

3) Red Sandstone and Marble Structures:

The fort predominantly comprises red sandstone structures, with white marble embellishments and inlays. Notable buildings, such as the Diwan-i-Am (Hall of Public Audience) and the Diwan-i-Khas (Hall of Private Audience), exemplify the exquisite blend of red sandstone and marble, featuring ornate carvings, delicate lattice work, and inlaid floral designs.

4) Palaces and Pavilions:

The fort houses several opulent palaces and pavilions that served as private residences and administrative centers for the Mughal rulers. The Jahangiri Mahal, built by Akbar for his Rajput wives, showcases a synthesis of Rajput and Mughal architectural styles with its angular balconies, ornate brackets, and intricate motifs.

5) Sheesh Mahal (Mirror Palace):

One of the striking structures within the fort is the Sheesh Mahal, a pavilion entirely adorned with intricate mirror work, reflecting the aesthetic brilliance of Mughal craftsmanship. The mirrored ceilings and walls create an illusion of an illuminated space, amplifying the visual grandeur.

6) **Jahangir's Hauz and Shahjahani Mahal:**

Jahangir's Hauz, a quadrangular tank within the fort complex, served as a reservoir. Nearby stands the Shahjahani Mahal, an elegant structure exhibiting architectural elements from the Shah Jahan era, characterized by delicate floral patterns and balconies overlooking the riverfront.

7) **Musamman Burj and Khas Mahal:**

The Musamman Burj, an octagonal tower, is a poignant structure where Shah Jahan was imprisoned by Aurangzeb. Adjacent to it stands the Khas Mahal, a white marble palace with elegant arches and intricate lattice screens, reflecting the refined taste of Shah Jahan's architectural vision.

8) **Gardens and Courtyards:**

Within the fort complex, various gardens and courtyards, such as the Anguri Bagh and the Machchhi Bhawan, offer serene landscapes, featuring symmetrically laid out gardens, water channels, and fountains, creating a tranquil ambiance amidst the imposing fortification.

9) **Strategic Features:**

The fort boasts strategic elements like bastions, moats, and defensive structures, emphasizing its military significance. The solid defensive walls, designed to withstand sieges, demonstrate the architectural ingenuity and defensive capabilities of the Mughal builders.

3.3.3 Fatehpur Sikri:

Fatehpur Sikri is a UNESCO World Heritage Site located near Agra, India. Built during the reign of Emperor Akbar in the late 16th century, it served as his capital for a short period. The complex boasts impressive Mughal architecture, including the Buland Darwaza and the Jama Masjid, and is known for its unique blend of Persian and Indian styles. Today, Fatehpur Sikri stands as a historical and architectural marvel, preserving the grandeur of the Mughal era.

1) **Historical Significance**:

Fatehpur Sikri, located near Agra in Uttar Pradesh, India, is a historic city built by Emperor Akbar in the late 16th century. It served as the capital of the Mughal Empire from 1571 to 1585 and is a UNESCO World Heritage Site, recognized for its historical and architectural importance.

2) **Akbar's Vision**:

Emperor Akbar, known for his innovative governance and religious tolerance, established Fatehpur Sikri as his new capital to commemorate his victory over the state of Gujarat and to create a place that embodied his ideals of unity and harmony among various religious communities.

3) **Architectural Marvel**:
Fatehpur Sikri is celebrated for its exquisite Mughal architecture, characterized by a fusion of Persian, Indian, and Islamic styles. The buildings in the city are predominantly made of red sandstone, and their intricate design and craftsmanship are a testament to the creative genius of the Mughal architects and artisans.

4) **Layout and Structures**:
The city of Fatehpur Sikri is laid out in a grid-like pattern with various buildings and courtyards. Key structures within the complex include the Buland Darwaza (Gate of Victory), Jama Masjid (Grand Mosque), Diwan-i-Khas (Hall of Private Audience), Diwan-i-Am (Hall of Public Audience), Panch Mahal, and the palaces of Akbar's queens, including Jodha Bai's Palace.

5) **Buland Darwaza**:
The Buland Darwaza, also known as the Gate of Victory, is one of the most iconic structures in Fatehpur Sikri. It stands at a height of 54 meters and is a grand entrance to the city. Inscriptions on the gate glorify Akbar's victory in Gujarat.

6) **Jama Masjid**:
The Jama Masjid in Fatehpur Sikri is one of the largest mosques in India and can accommodate thousands of worshippers. Its central courtyard and prayer hall are adorned with intricate carvings and marble inlays, showcasing the Mughal architectural finesse.

7) **Diwan-i-Khas**:
The Diwan-i-Khas, or Hall of Private Audience, is where Akbar met his select courtiers and held private discussions. Its distinctive feature is the central pillar, which originally held Akbar's famous "peacock throne." The building is beautifully decorated with intricate designs and motifs.

8) **Diwan-i-Am**:
The Diwan-i-Am, or Hall of Public Audience, is a large open pavilion where the emperor addressed the general public. It features a prominent throne alcove with a decorative canopy. The courtyard is surrounded by colonnades and adorned with ornate columns.

9) **Panch Mahal**:
The Panch Mahal, or "Five-story Palace," is an intriguing structure with an open design. It is said to have served as a pleasure pavilion for the ladies of the court and offers panoramic views of the surrounding area from its top floor.

10) **Abandonment and Preservation**:
Fatehpur Sikri was abandoned as a capital in 1585, primarily due to water scarcity and the threat of conflict. However, it remains remarkably well-preserved to this day, offering visitors a glimpse into the splendor of the Mughal era and its architectural innovations.

3.3.4 Allahabad Fort:

Allahabad Fort, situated in Allahabad, India, is a historic fort built during the reign of Emperor Akbar in the late 16th century. It is strategically located at the confluence of the Ganges and Yamuna rivers, known as the Sangam. The fort's architecture showcases Mughal style with its distinctive red sandstone walls and grand entrance. While it is no longer in use as a military fortification, it stands as a historical monument, attracting visitors for its architectural beauty and historical significance.

1) **Historical Significance**:

   The Allahabad Fort, located in the city of Allahabad in the Indian state of Uttar Pradesh, is a historic fort that holds immense historical and architectural significance. It stands at the confluence of the Ganges and Yamuna rivers, a sacred site known as the Sangam.

2) **Construction During Akbar's Reign**:

   The construction of the Allahabad Fort was commissioned by Emperor Akbar in 1583. Akbar was known for his interest in architecture and had several forts and structures built across his empire.

3) **Strategic Location**:

   The fort was strategically positioned at the confluence of two major rivers, serving as a significant military and administrative center. Its location made it a vital outpost for the Mughal Empire's control over the region.

4) **Architectural Style**:

   The Allahabad Fort is a fine example of Mughal architecture. It is primarily constructed using red sandstone, a common feature of Mughal structures. The fort's design exhibits a fusion of Indian, Persian, and Islamic architectural styles.

5) **Layout and Structures**:

   The fort is rectangular in shape and covers a vast area. It is surrounded by high walls and bastions, showcasing its defensive purpose. Inside the fort, there are various structures, including palaces, mosques, gardens, and administrative buildings.

6) **Akbar's Palace**:

   One of the notable structures within the fort is Akbar's Palace, which served as the emperor's residence during his visits to Allahabad. It features intricately designed chambers and halls, with ornate decorations.

7) **Patalpuri Temple**:

   Located within the fort complex is the Patalpuri Temple, which is a significant religious site for Hindus. It is believed to be one of the oldest temples in Allahabad and is dedicated to Lord Rama.

8) **The Saraswati Koop**:

Another religious site within the fort is the Saraswati Koop, a well that is considered sacred. According to Hindu mythology, this well is believed to be connected to the mythical Saraswati River.

9) **British Occupation and Preservation**:

During the British colonial period, the Allahabad Fort played a role in the events of the Indian Rebellion of 1857. It was used as a military garrison and later as a prison. Today, the fort is preserved as a historical monument and is under the care of the Archaeological Survey of India.

10) **Tourist Attraction**:

The Allahabad Fort is a popular tourist destination, attracting visitors interested in history and architecture. Its location at the Sangam, where the Ganges, Yamuna, and mythical Saraswati rivers converge, adds to its significance as a pilgrimage site. The fort is also known for hosting the Kumbh Mela, one of the largest religious gatherings in the world, which takes place every 12 years.

3.3.5 Lahore Fort:

The Lahore Fort, situated in Lahore, Pakistan, is a historic Mughal fort that dates back to the 11th century. Renowned for its stunning architecture, it showcases a fusion of Mughal, Persian, and Sikh influences. The fort encompasses various palaces, gardens, and iconic structures, including the Sheesh Mahal (Palace of Mirrors). Recognized as a UNESCO World Heritage Site, it stands as a symbol of Pakistan's rich cultural heritage and architectural brilliance..

1) **Historical Significance**:

The Lahore Fort, located in Lahore, Pakistan, is a historic fort with a rich and storied past. It has played a pivotal role in the history of the region, witnessing the rise and fall of various dynasties and empires.

2) **Origins and Early History**:

The origins of the Lahore Fort date back to antiquity. The earliest historical references suggest that a mud fort existed on the site as early as the 11th century during the Ghaznavid period. Subsequent rulers, including the Ghurids and the Delhi Sultanate, expanded and renovated the fort.

3) **Mughal Era**:

The most significant phase of the Lahore Fort's history occurred during the Mughal Empire. Emperor Akbar rebuilt and expanded the fort, transforming it into a magnificent structure in the late 16th century. It served as a prominent seat of Mughal power in the region.

4) **Architectural Marvel**:

The Lahore Fort is celebrated for its architectural splendor. It exhibits a blend of Mughal, Persian, Islamic, and indigenous architectural styles. The extensive use of red sandstone and marble, intricate tile work, and decorative motifs make it a masterpiece of Mughal architecture.

5) **Structures within the Fort**:

The fort complex is vast and includes various structures such as the Sheesh Mahal (Palace of Mirrors), Diwan-i-Aam (Hall of Public Audience), Diwan-i-Khas (Hall of Private Audience), Naulakha Pavilion, and the Jahangir Quadrangle. Each structure within the fort is a testament to Mughal craftsmanship and creativity.

6) **Sheesh Mahal**:

The Sheesh Mahal is one of the most iconic features of the Lahore Fort. It is known for its exquisite mirror work, intricate frescoes, and beautiful floral patterns. The palace was built by Shah Jahan, the famous Mughal emperor, and it reflects his penchant for opulent architecture.

7) **Jahangir Quadrangle**:

This quadrangle was constructed during the reign of Emperor Jahangir. It features a splendid gateway and several buildings, including the Akbari Sarai and the Kala Burj. The Akbari Sarai, in particular, is a striking structure with its beautifully arched gateways and galleries.

8) **Sikh and British Period**:

The Lahore Fort saw significant changes during the Sikh and British periods. The Sikhs, under Maharaja Ranjit Singh, captured Lahore in the early 19th century and made alterations to the fort. Later, during British rule, the fort was used for military purposes.

9) **UNESCO World Heritage Site**:

In recognition of its historical and architectural significance, the Lahore Fort was designated as a UNESCO World Heritage Site in 1981. This international recognition has played a crucial role in the preservation and conservation of the fort's heritage.

10) **Modern-Day Attraction**:

Today, the Lahore Fort is a popular tourist destination, attracting visitors from around the world. Its well-preserved structures, lush gardens, and the fusion of various architectural styles provide a captivating glimpse into the grandeur of the Mughal era and the rich history of the Indian subcontinent.

3.4 Jahangir:

Jahangir, also known as Nur-ud-din Muhammad Salim, was the fourth ruler of the Mughal Empire, reigning from 1605 to 1627. His reign is often characterized as a period of cultural flourishing and religious tolerance, marked by the convergence of art, literature, and politics. During the reign of Emperor Jahangir, Mughal art and architecture witnessed a distinctive evolution, marked by specific features that characterized this period of cultural richness and artistic refinement:

1) **Floral and Natural Motifs:**
   Jahangir's era embraced a fascination for nature, evident in art. Paintings depicted landscapes, flowers, birds, and animals in intricate detail, reflecting a deep appreciation for the beauty of the natural world.

2) **Mughal Miniature Paintings:**
   The period saw the refinement and advancement of miniature painting as a distinct art form. Artists created highly detailed and delicately painted miniatures, often illustrating court scenes, portraits, and mythological themes with vibrant colors and meticulous precision.

3) **Naturalistic Portrayals:**
   Jahangir encouraged artists to depict naturalistic and realistic portrayals in art, emphasizing accurate depictions of flora, fauna, and human figures. This led to a departure from the stylized representations seen in earlier Mughal art.

4) **European Influence:**
   Jahangir's reign saw increased interaction with European cultures, which influenced Mughal art. European styles and techniques, especially in portraiture and perspective, found their way into Mughal paintings.

5) **Emphasis on Portraiture:**
   Jahangir's interest in portraiture led to the development of lifelike and detailed portraits. Artists captured the emperor's likeness, as well as that of other notable figures in the court, with remarkable accuracy.

6) **Architectural Patronage:**
   Jahangir continued the patronage of architectural projects, contributing to the construction and renovation of buildings. Notable examples include the Shah Jahan-built Tomb of Itmad-ud-Daula in Agra, known for its intricate pietra dura work and delicate marble carvings.

7) **Liberal Patronage of Artists:**
   Jahangir was a patron of the arts, providing encouragement and support to artists. His court attracted talented painters, calligraphers, and artisans, fostering a creative environment that contributed to the flourishing of art and craftsmanship.

8) **Jahangir's Album (Jahangirnama):**
   The emperor himself was an artist and maintained a personal album known as the Jahangirnama, where he documented events, made sketches, and penned his thoughts. This manuscript reflects Jahangir's artistic inclinations and serves as a valuable historical and artistic record.

9) Continuation of Mughal Architectural Styles:

While Jahangir's reign did not witness significant architectural innovations, his support sustained the architectural styles established by his predecessors, further embellishing existing structures and monuments.

10) Cultural Synthesis:

Jahangir's era was characterized by cultural syncretism, encompassing diverse influences from Persian, Indian, and European artistic traditions. This blending of cultures and artistic styles contributed to the richness and diversity of Mughal art and architecture during his reign.

3.4.1 Sikandara:

Sikandara, near Agra, India, is famous for the mausoleum of Akbar the Great, the third Mughal emperor. The mausoleum showcases Mughal architecture with its red sandstone and white marble design. It is set within a beautiful Persian-style garden and features an imposing Buland Darwaza (gateway). Sikandara's serene ambiance and historical importance make it a revered site for tourists and history enthusiasts alike.

1) Historical Significance:

Sikandara is a historic town located near Agra, Uttar Pradesh, India. It is renowned for being the final resting place of the third Mughal emperor, Akbar the Great. His mausoleum, known as Sikandara or Sikandara Akbarabad, is a prominent architectural and historical landmark.

2) Akbar's Reign:

Akbar ruled the Mughal Empire from 1556 to 1605 and is widely regarded as one of the greatest emperors in Indian history. During his reign, he expanded the empire's territory, implemented administrative reforms, and promoted religious tolerance and cultural diversity.

3) Construction of the Mausoleum:

Akbar began the construction of his mausoleum during his lifetime, and it was completed after his death in 1605 during the reign of his son, Jahangir. The mausoleum reflects Akbar's eclectic taste in architecture, drawing inspiration from various cultural influences.

4) Architectural Style:

Sikandara's architectural style is a blend of Persian, Indian, and Central Asian influences. The mausoleum's design features red sandstone and white marble, characteristic of Mughal architecture. Its symmetrical layout and decorative elements make it an early example of the Mughal architectural style that would later reach its zenith with the Taj Mahal.

5) **Buland Darwaza**:

The entrance to Sikandara is marked by the Buland Darwaza, a grand and imposing gateway. This towering structure showcases Persian and Mughal architectural elements and serves as the main entrance to the mausoleum complex.

6) **Chhatris**:

Sikandara is known for its chhatris, which are elevated dome-shaped pavilions. These chhatris are a prominent feature in the Mughal architectural tradition and can be seen throughout the mausoleum complex, adding to its visual appeal.

7) **Garden Complex**:

The mausoleum is surrounded by a beautiful garden complex, which includes lush lawns, pathways, and water channels. The Persian-style gardens, known as chahar bagh, are divided into four quadrants, symbolizing paradise on Earth, a common theme in Mughal garden design.

8) **Tomb Chamber**:

The central structure of the mausoleum houses Akbar's tomb. The tomb chamber is simple and unadorned, in keeping with Akbar's preference for simplicity in death. The cenotaph of Akbar is placed in the center, and visitors can pay their respects here.

9) **Influence on Later Monuments**:

Sikandara's design and layout had a profound influence on subsequent Mughal architectural projects, particularly the construction of the Taj Mahal in Agra. The Taj Mahal, built by Akbar's grandson Shah Jahan, bears similarities in its use of white marble, symmetry, and garden layout.

10) **Preservation and UNESCO World Heritage Site**:

Sikandara and its mausoleum have been well-preserved over the centuries. In 1993, it was designated as a UNESCO World Heritage Site, recognizing its cultural and historical significance. This recognition has helped protect and promote the legacy of Akbar and Mughal architecture.

3.4.2 Tomb of Itmad-ud-Daula:

The Tomb of Itimad-ud-Daulah, situated in Agra, India, is a historic mausoleum often called the "Baby Taj" due to its intricate white marble design and delicate pietra dura inlay work. Built between 1622 and 1628 by Empress Nur Jahan in memory of her father, it's considered a precursor to the Taj Mahal's architectural grandeur. Set in a charbagh garden, it showcases delicate floral and geometric patterns, making it a captivating example of Mughal architecture and craftsmanship. Following are the key points of itmad-ud-Daula:

1) **Historical Significance**:
The Tomb of Itimad-ud-Daulah, also known as the "Baby Taj," is a historic mausoleum located in Agra, Uttar Pradesh, India. It holds significant historical and architectural importance as one of the early Mughal-era tombs.

2) **Built in Memory**:
The mausoleum was constructed between 1622 and 1628 by Empress Nur Jahan, the wife of Emperor Jahangir, in memory of her father, Mirza Ghiyas Beg, who held the title of "Itimad-ud-Daulah," which translates to "Pillar of the State."

3) **Architectural Style**:
The Tomb of Itimad-ud-Daulah is considered a precursor to the Taj Mahal and is known for its intricate and delicate architectural style. It represents a transition between the earlier Mughal architecture and the more elaborative style seen in the Taj Mahal.

4) **White Marble Beauty**:
The mausoleum is constructed primarily from white marble, which lends it a stunning appearance, especially when illuminated by the soft glow of the sun. It is often referred to as the "Jewel Box" due to its delicate and ornate design.

5) **Garden Setting**:
The tomb is set within a charbagh (fourfold garden) layout, a Persian-style garden with quadrants divided by pathways and water channels. The garden adds to the tranquility and aesthetic appeal of the mausoleum.

6) **Tomb's Design**:
The central tomb structure is square in shape and features a central chamber containing the cenotaphs of Itimad-ud-Daulah and his wife, Asmat Begum. The chamber is surrounded by an intricately designed screen carved from marble, allowing visitors to view the cenotaphs.

7) **Intricate Inlay Work**:
The most remarkable feature of the tomb is its intricate inlay work, known as pietra dura. The tomb's walls and surfaces are adorned with delicate floral and geometric designs created by setting semi-precious stones like lapis lazuli, onyx, carnelian, and turquoise into the marble.

8) **Motifs and Patterns**:
The pietra dura work at the Tomb of Itimad-ud-Daulah includes motifs such as vines, flowers, and Islamic calligraphy. The combination of these elements creates a harmonious and aesthetically pleasing design.

9) **Historical Influence**:
The delicate design and inlay work seen at the Tomb of Itimad-ud-Daulah had a significant influence on subsequent Mughal architecture, particularly in the design and decoration of the Taj Mahal, which was built by Shah Jahan, the grandson of Emperor Akbar.

10) Tourist Attraction:

Today, the Tomb of Itimad-ud-Daulah is a popular tourist attraction in Agra. Visitors come to appreciate its architectural beauty, serene garden, and the historical significance it holds in the development of Mughal architecture. It is often regarded as a precursor to the grandeur of the Taj Mahal and serves as a testament to the Mughal Empire's artistic and cultural legacy.

3.5 Shahjahan:

Shah Jahan, the fifth Mughal emperor, reigned from 1628 to 1658 and is renowned for commissioning the Taj Mahal, an iconic symbol of love and architectural splendor. His rule marked a "Golden Age of Mughal Architecture," with structures like the Red Fort and Jama Masjid. Shah Jahan's reign was marked by a culmination of artistic opulence, architectural magnificence, and the zenith of Mughal cultural refinement. Here are the defining features of art and architecture during his rule:

1) Mughal Architecture at its Zenith:

Shah Jahan's era witnessed the pinnacle of Mughal architecture, exemplified by iconic structures like the Taj Mahal, Agra Fort, and the Jama Masjid in Delhi.

2) Taj Mahal - Epitome of Mughal Architecture:

The Taj Mahal stands as the epitome of Shah Jahan's architectural legacy, showcasing intricate marble inlay work, symmetrical gardens, and a harmonious blend of Persian, Indian, and Islamic architectural elements.

3) Extravagant Use of Marble:

Shah Jahan's buildings were characterized by the extensive use of white marble, symbolizing purity and grandeur. Marble structures with intricate carvings and delicate pietra dura embellishments were prominent.

4) Symmetry and Precision:

Architectural features displayed meticulous symmetry and precision, reflecting a highly refined sense of balance and aesthetics. This perfection is evident in the Taj Mahal's symmetrical layout and detailed ornamentation.

5) Red Fort and Palaces:

Shah Jahan commissioned the Red Fort in Delhi, a colossal fortress showcasing impressive palaces like the Diwan-i-Khas and the Diwan-i-Am, adorned with marble, semi-precious stones, and fine carvings.

6) Innovative Engineering:

Shah Jahan's architects and engineers showcased innovative construction techniques, evident in the colossal domes, intricate lattice work, and precise geometry seen in structures like the Taj Mahal and Red Fort.

7) **Jama Masjid, Delhi:**
The construction of the Jama Masjid in Delhi, one of the largest mosques in India, reflects Shah Jahan's architectural patronage, featuring imposing domes, slender minarets, and extensive use of red sandstone and white marble.

8) **Artistic Patronage:**
Shah Jahan continued the tradition of patronizing arts, including miniature paintings, calligraphy, and decorative arts. Court ateliers flourished, producing exquisite artworks depicting court life, landscapes, and portraits.

9) **Integration of Gemstones:**
The use of gemstones, including lapis lazuli, agate, and carnelian, in intricate inlay work, added to the opulence of Mughal architecture during Shah Jahan's reign.

10) **Cultural Fusion and Legacy:**
Shah Jahan's architectural legacy epitomized a fusion of diverse cultural elements, creating an enduring legacy that continues to influence and inspire architects, artists, and admirers worldwide.

3.5.1 The Taj Mahal:

The Taj Mahal, located in Agra, India, is an iconic white marble mausoleum commissioned by Emperor Shah Jahan in memory of his beloved wife Mumtaz Mahal. Completed in 1653, it is renowned for its symmetrical beauty, intricate pietra dura inlay work, and stunning architecture. The Taj Mahal is considered one of the world's most celebrated monuments and a UNESCO World Heritage Site, symbolizing eternal love.

A) **Architectural Features of Tajmahal:**
The Taj Mahal encompasses a symmetrical layout within a vast complex. It features the main mausoleum, a mosque, a guesthouse, lush gardens, reflecting pools, and intricate pathways. The entire complex spans approximately 42 acres and is enclosed by high walls on three sides, with the river forming a natural boundary.

1) **Mausoleum Structure:**
The central structure, the mausoleum, stands as the focal point of the complex. It consists of a massive white marble dome atop a square base, flanked by four slender minarets at each corner, creating a striking silhouette against the sky.

2) **Architectural Symmetry:**
The Taj Mahal exhibits meticulous symmetry in its design, reflecting a perfect balance in every aspect, from the placement of minarets to the garden's layout. This symmetry symbolizes harmony and precision in Mughal architecture.

3) **Marble Inlay and Pietra Dura:**
The façade is adorned with exquisite marble inlay work, known as pietra dura, featuring intricate floral patterns, calligraphy, and geometric designs crafted from semi-precious stones like jasper, jade, and lapis lazuli. This delicate work embellishes the marble surface, creating an ethereal play of light and color.

4) Main Dome:

The colossal central dome, reaching a height of around 73 meters (240 feet), is a hallmark of Mughal architecture. Its onion-shaped design, crowned by a lotus finial, symbolizes divine beauty and spirituality.

5) Decorative Elements:

The exterior and interior of the mausoleum are adorned with ornate carvings, arabesques, verses from the Quran, and intricate geometric patterns. The use of delicate jali screens and marble lattice work allows sunlight to filter in, creating a mesmerizing interplay of light and shadow.

6) Reflecting Pools and Gardens:

The charbagh (quadrilateral) garden layout with symmetrical pathways and reflecting pools, aligned with the mausoleum's axis, symbolizes paradise in Islamic architecture. The gardens, adorned with fountains and flora, evoke a sense of tranquility and serenity.

7) Red Sandstone Base:

The Taj Mahal's base, constructed with red sandstone, provides a contrast to the luminous white marble structure. The intricate patterns and carvings on the base complement the grandeur of the marble edifice.

8) Environmental Adaptations:

The Taj Mahal's architectural design includes features like air wells, water channels, and ventilation systems to regulate the internal temperature and mitigate the effects of environmental factors, showcasing ingenious engineering solutions.

9) Change of Color: T

The Taj Mahal displays a subtle change in color throughout the day, glowing pinkish at dawn, pristine white during the day, and taking on a golden hue at sunset, owing to the play of light and atmospheric conditions.

B) Historical Importance of Tajmahal:

The Taj Mahal, a UNESCO World Heritage Site and one of the most iconic structures globally, stands as a testament to love, architectural brilliance, and cultural heritage. Its historical importance spans centuries, encapsulating diverse facets that have contributed to its status as a symbol of India's rich history and heritage.

1) Commissioning and Construction:

Commissioned by Emperor Shah Jahan in 1632 in memory of his beloved wife Mumtaz Mahal, the Taj Mahal's construction took around 20 years and employed thousands of skilled artisans, craftsmen, and laborers. The monument stands on the banks of the Yamuna River in Agra, India, reflecting an unparalleled architectural and artistic endeavor.

2) **Symbol of Eternal Love:**
At its core, the Taj Mahal symbolizes the eternal love between Shah Jahan and Mumtaz Mahal. Its construction is a poignant testimony to the emperor's grief and enduring love for his wife, immortalizing their love story through a magnificent architectural marvel.

3) **Architectural Grandeur:**
The Taj Mahal exemplifies the zenith of Mughal architecture, blending diverse elements from Persian, Islamic, Indian, and Turkish architectural styles. Its structural perfection, intricate carvings, delicate marble inlay work, and symmetrical design represent the pinnacle of architectural brilliance.

4) **Cultural Syncretism:**
The Taj Mahal stands as an epitome of cultural synthesis, showcasing a harmonious blend of various artistic traditions and cultural influences prevalent during the Mughal era. Its design reflects the convergence of diverse cultural elements into a singular masterpiece.

5) **Historical Legacy:**
Beyond its role as a monument to love, the Taj Mahal bears historical significance as a witness to the Mughal Empire's cultural and architectural zenith. It symbolizes the opulence, power, and grandeur of the Mughal rulers and serves as a tangible representation of India's rich historical tapestry.

6) **Global Architectural Marvel:**
The Taj Mahal's architectural brilliance transcends borders, captivating people worldwide and earning its recognition as one of the seven wonders of the modern world. Its universal appeal attracts millions of visitors annually, contributing significantly to global cultural heritage.

7) **UNESCO World Heritage Site:**
In 1983, the Taj Mahal was designated as a UNESCO World Heritage Site, acknowledging its outstanding universal value, cultural significance, and historical importance. This recognition solidified its place among the world's most revered cultural landmarks.

8) **Economic and Tourism Impact:**
The Taj Mahal has played a pivotal role in boosting tourism and economic development in India. It remains a major tourist attraction, drawing visitors, scholars, and admirers from diverse backgrounds, contributing significantly to the local and national economy.

9) **Conservation and Restoration Efforts:**
Various conservation and restoration initiatives have been undertaken to preserve the Taj Mahal's architectural integrity and beauty. These efforts highlight its significance as a heritage site and emphasize the importance of safeguarding cultural treasures for future generations.

10) Symbol of National Pride:

The Taj Mahal serves as a symbol of national pride for India, representing the country's rich history, cultural heritage, and architectural excellence. It embodies the spirit of India's cultural diversity and artistic legacy, evoking a sense of pride and admiration among its citizens.

3.5.2 Red Fort:

The Red Fort, located in Delhi, India, is a historic fort and UNESCO World Heritage Site. Built by Emperor Shah Jahan in the mid-17th century, it is an architectural masterpiece known for its stunning red sandstone walls and intricate marble inlay work. The fort served as the main residence of the Mughal emperors for over two centuries and is a symbol of India's rich history and cultural heritage. Today, it is a popular tourist attraction, attracting visitors from around the world.

A) Architectural features of Red Fort:

The Red Fort, an iconic symbol of India's rich cultural heritage and historical significance, stands as a testament to Mughal architectural brilliance and imperial grandeur. Commissioned by Emperor Shah Jahan in 1638, the fort served as the primary residence of the Mughal emperors until 1857. Its architectural features, strategic design, and historical legacy showcase a blend of Persian, Timurid, and Indian architectural styles.

1) Historical Background:

Commissioned during Shah Jahan's reign, the Red Fort's construction began in 1638 and took nearly a decade to complete. Situated in Delhi, it was originally known as "Qila-e-Mubarak" or the Blessed Fort, serving as the seat of the Mughal Empire.

2) Architectural Layout and Design:

The Red Fort spans over 250 acres, enclosed by massive red sandstone walls reaching up to 33 meters in height. The fortification walls, extending for around 2.5 kilometers, encompass numerous structures, pavilions, gardens, and administrative buildings within its complex.

3) Red Sandstone Construction:

The fort's distinct red sandstone walls, from which it derives its name, were built with meticulous craftsmanship. The use of red sandstone as the primary building material provided durability and a striking appearance, reflecting the architectural grandeur of the Mughal era.

4) Chatta Chowk (Covered Bazaar):

The fort's entrance, known as the Lahori Gate, leads to Chatta Chowk, a covered market street lined with arched cells that once housed various artisans, craftsmen, and merchants. This marketplace reflects the economic and cultural vibrancy of the Mughal period.

5) **Diwan-i-Am (Hall of Public Audience):**

One of the prominent structures within the Red Fort is the Diwan-i-Am, a majestic hall where the emperor held public audiences. The hall features elegant arches, marble columns, and a raised platform adorned with intricate marble inlay work.

6) **Diwan-i-Khas (Hall of Private Audience):**

The Diwan-i-Khas served as the emperor's private audience hall, adorned with exquisite white marble, intricate floral designs, and an iconic throne platform known as the Takht-i-Murassa. This platform was where the emperor conducted private meetings.

7) **Rang Mahal (Palace of Colors):**

The Rang Mahal was the residence of the emperor's wives and concubines, featuring vibrant paintings, mirrored ceilings, and decorative embellishments. The palace's design symbolized opulence and luxury, showcasing the imperial lifestyle.

8) **Khas Mahal (Private Palace):**

The Khas Mahal, an elegant marble palace, served as the emperor's private residence. It comprises exquisite marble carvings, arched openings, ornate jali screens, and a centrally located marble fountain, exuding refinement and grace.

9) **Mumtaz Mahal (Palace of Mumtaz):**

Named after Shah Jahan's beloved wife, Mumtaz Mahal was a residential palace featuring delicately carved marble screens, water channels, and landscaped gardens, creating a serene ambiance for the royal family.

10) **Moti Masjid (Pearl Mosque):**

The Moti Masjid, a pristine white marble mosque within the fort complex, exemplifies architectural elegance with its three domes, minarets, and intricate carvings. It served as a private place of worship for the imperial family.

11) **Zenana (Royal Apartments):**

The Zenana, or women's quarters, housed the royal ladies and their attendants. It comprised multiple palaces, courtyards, and gardens, reflecting a blend of privacy, luxury, and architectural finesse.

12) **Nahr-i-Bihisht (Stream of Paradise):**

The Nahr-i-Bihisht, a central water channel, divided the fort complex into formal gardens, reflecting the Charbagh (quadrilateral garden) style, reminiscent of Islamic paradise gardens.

B) **Historical importance of Red Fort:**

The Red Fort, also known as Lal Qila, is a historic monument in Delhi, India, renowned for its architectural grandeur, cultural significance, and role as a symbol of India's rich heritage. Built during the Mughal era, it holds immense historical importance owing to its association with significant events, architectural splendor, and its status as a witness to pivotal moments in India's history.

1) **Foundation and Construction:**
Commissioned by Emperor Shah Jahan in 1638, the Red Fort's construction took nearly a decade to complete. Situated along the banks of the Yamuna River, the fort was designed as the primary residence of the Mughal emperors.

2) **Architectural Significance:**
The Red Fort represents the zenith of Mughal architecture, blending Persian, Timurid, and Indian architectural styles. Its distinctive red sandstone walls, reaching up to 33 meters in height, and expansive complex showcase the opulence and grandeur of the Mughal era.

3) **Strategic Location:**
Built on a strategic location, the Red Fort served as the center of governance and military operations for the Mughal Empire. Its fortified walls and strategic design made it a symbol of power and authority.

4) **Imperial Residences and Pavilions:**
The fort's complex houses numerous structures, including the Diwan-i-Am (Hall of Public Audience) and Diwan-i-Khas (Hall of Private Audience), where the emperor conducted official affairs and met with dignitaries. The Rang Mahal, Khas Mahal, and other palaces within the fort served as royal residences, showcasing exquisite Mughal architectural finesse.

5) **Cultural Significance:**
The Red Fort is not only an architectural marvel but also a symbol of cultural synthesis. The fort's Chatta Chowk, a covered market street, housed artisans and traders, reflecting the economic and cultural vibrancy of the Mughal era.

6) **Historical Events:**
The fort witnessed significant historical events, including the iconic speech delivered by India's first Prime Minister, Jawaharlal Nehru, on August 15, 1947, marking India's independence from British colonial rule. The Red Fort became the site of the annual Independence Day celebrations, further solidifying its historical importance.

7) **Symbol of National Identity:**
The Red Fort holds immense significance as a symbol of India's national identity. Its association with India's struggle for independence and subsequent independence celebrations has embedded it deeply in the national consciousness.

8) **UNESCO World Heritage Site:**
In 2007, the Red Fort was designated as a UNESCO World Heritage Site, acknowledging its outstanding universal value, cultural significance, and historical importance. This recognition elevated its global stature and highlighted its role in world heritage.

9) **Tourist Attraction and Cultural Hub:**
The Red Fort is a major tourist attraction, drawing visitors from across the globe to marvel at its architectural splendor and immerse them in India's rich history. The fort

serves as a cultural hub, hosting events, exhibitions, and cultural programs that showcase India's heritage.

10) Preservation and Conservation Efforts:

Various preservation and conservation initiatives have been undertaken to safeguard the Red Fort's architectural integrity and cultural legacy. These efforts emphasize the importance of preserving historical monuments for future generations.

3.5.3 Jama Masjid:

The Jama Masjid, located in Old Delhi, India, is one of the largest and most magnificent mosques in the world. Built by the Mughal Emperor Shah Jahan between 1644 and 1656, it can accommodate up to 25,000 worshippers. Its stunning architecture features red sandstone and white marble, and it boasts three grand domes, two minarets, and a vast courtyard. The Jama Masjid stands as an architectural and cultural gem, symbolizing the Mughal era's grandeur and religious significance. Following are the key points of jama masjid:

1) Historical Significance:

The Jama Masjid, also known as the "Masjid-i-Jahan-Numa," is one of the largest and most significant mosques in India. It is located in Old Delhi and holds immense historical and religious importance.

2) Construction by Shah Jahan:

The Jama Masjid was commissioned by the Mughal Emperor Shah Jahan, the same ruler responsible for the Taj Mahal and the Red Fort. Its construction began in 1650 and was completed in 1656. It was designed by the architect Ustad Khalil.

3) Architectural Style:

The mosque is an architectural masterpiece that reflects the grandeur of Mughal architecture. It is constructed using red sandstone and white marble, creating a stunning visual contrast. The mosque's design incorporates elements of Persian and Indian architectural styles.

4) Dome and Minarets:

The Jama Masjid features three grand domes made of white marble, along with two towering minarets. The central dome is the largest, measuring 80 feet in height. The minarets, each standing 130 feet tall, provide a striking visual presence.

5) Courtyard:

The mosque is built around a vast courtyard that can accommodate thousands of worshippers. The courtyard is paved with red sandstone and is an integral part of the mosque's layout. It is an open space that allows for congregational prayers and gatherings.

6) **Prayer Hall**:

The main prayer hall of the Jama Masjid is equally impressive, with a high ceiling adorned with floral motifs and inscriptions from the Quran. The hall can accommodate a large number of worshippers and is a place for communal prayers.

7) **Inlay Work**:

Like many Mughal structures, the Jama Masjid features intricate inlay work using white marble. The mosque's façade and interior walls are adorned with floral and calligraphic designs, adding to its aesthetic appeal.

8) **Buland Darwaza**:

The mosque's entrance is marked by a grand gateway known as the Buland Darwaza. This imposing structure is made of red sandstone and features arches, niches, and calligraphic inscriptions.

9) **Historical and Religious Significance**:

The Jama Masjid holds significant religious importance for Muslims in Delhi and across India. It is not only a place of worship but also a symbol of Islamic heritage and cultural heritage.

10) **Tourist Attraction**:

The Jama Masjid is a popular tourist destination, attracting visitors from around the world who come to admire its architectural splendor, explore its rich history, and experience the tranquility of the mosque's courtyard. Climbing one of the minarets provides breathtaking panoramic views of Old Delhi.

3.6 Mughal Painting:

Mughal painting is a rich and intricate artistic tradition that flourished in India during the Mughal Empire, primarily from the 16th to the 19th century. It is characterized by its exquisite detail, vivid colors, and a fusion of diverse artistic influences. Following are the key points about the mughal paintings:

1) **Historical Context**:

Mughal painting emerged during the Mughal Empire, which ruled over India from the early 16th to the mid-19th century. This period saw a fusion of Persian, Indian, and Central Asian cultures, which greatly influenced Mughal art, including painting.

2) **Persian Influence**:

Persian artists, scholars, and poets were welcomed at the Mughal court, and their artistic techniques and styles had a profound impact on Mughal painting. This influence is evident in the use of Persian motifs, calligraphy, and manuscript illumination.

3) **Akbar's Patronage**:

The Mughal Emperor Akbar was a significant patron of the arts, and during his reign (1556-1605), Mughal painting underwent a significant transformation. Akbar's atelier, or royal workshop, attracted talented artists who worked on various projects, including the Hamzanama and Akbarnama manuscripts.

4) **Naturalistic Style**:
Mughal paintings are characterized by a naturalistic style that aimed to depict subjects accurately. Artists paid close attention to detail, using vivid colors and intricate brushwork to create lifelike representations of flora, fauna, and human figures.

5) **Miniature Format**:
Mughal paintings are typically small in size and are known as miniatures. These miniatures were often created as part of manuscripts, illustrating scenes from literature, history, and mythology. The small format allowed for meticulous attention to detail.

6) **Themes and Subjects**:
Mughal paintings covered a wide range of themes, including portraits of emperors and courtiers, hunting scenes, court life, religious narratives, and Persian epics. Each theme conveyed different aspects of Mughal culture and society.

7) **Hunting Scenes**:
One of the recurring themes in Mughal painting is hunting scenes, reflecting the royal fascination with the sport. These paintings often depict the emperor and his entourage engaged in hunting expeditions, showcasing both the hunt itself and the wildlife of India.

8) **Religious and Mythological Themes**:
Mughal painters also illustrated religious and mythological narratives, such as scenes from the Ramayana and Mahabharata. These artworks reflected the religious diversity of the Mughal Empire and their interest in Indian culture.

9) **Portraiture**:
Mughal emperors were keen patrons of portraiture, leading to the creation of numerous lifelike portraits. These portraits provided a glimpse into the appearance and personalities of the rulers, offering insights into the Mughal court.

10) **Later Developments**:
Mughal painting continued to evolve under successive emperors, including Jahangir, Shah Jahan, and Aurangzeb. Jahangir, for example, was known for his interest in natural history and commissioned paintings of flora and fauna.

11) **Decline and Revival**:
The decline of the Mughal Empire in the 18th century resulted in a decline in the patronage of Mughal painting. However, it later saw a revival under the British Raj, as Indian artists began to adapt Mughal techniques to new themes and styles.

12) **Legacy and Influence**:
Mughal painting has left a lasting legacy on Indian art. It influenced various regional schools of painting, such as the Rajput, Pahari, and Deccani schools. Additionally,

Mughal miniature painting techniques continue to inspire contemporary Indian artists, and the art form remains an integral part of India's cultural heritage.

3.7 Regional Art and Architecture:

Regional art and architecture encompass a vast array of distinctive styles, techniques, and traditions that have evolved in specific geographic areas and cultural contexts. These artistic and architectural expressions are deeply rooted in the history, environment, and cultural heritage of their respective regions, reflecting the unique identities and influences that have shaped them over centuries. Regional art and architecture offer insights into the cultural, social, and historical aspects of different parts of the world.

3.7.1 Regional Art:

Regional art is a captivating reflection of cultural identity, historical narratives, and societal values across different parts of the world. Spanning centuries and continents, regional art movements have not only showcased remarkable creativity but also encapsulated the essence of diverse civilizations.

1) **Diversity in Regional Art:**
   Medieval India witnessed a rich diversity of artistic expressions across various regions. The diversity was deeply rooted in local cultures, traditions, and the patronage of ruling dynasties. From the intricately carved temples of the South to the vibrant miniature paintings of the Rajputs, each region showcased distinct artistic styles, mediums, and themes. This diversity allowed for a myriad of techniques and materials to flourish, contributing to the cultural richness of the subcontinent.

2) **Patronage by Regional Dynasties:**
   Regional rulers played a pivotal role in nurturing and promoting indigenous art forms. Dynasties like the Cholas, Vijayanagara Empire, and Rajputs were significant patrons, commissioning artworks that reflected their cultural and political identities. Their patronage not only encouraged artists but also led to the development of unique artistic traditions specific to each region.

3) **Influence of Religious Beliefs:**
   Religion served as a major influence on regional art. In South India, temple art was a focal point, embodying devotion to various deities through intricate stone carvings and sculptures narrating mythological stories. The artistic expressions in different regions were often intertwined with religious narratives and beliefs, reflecting the spiritual ethos prevalent in those areas.

4) **Distinct Architectural Styles:**
   Regional architecture exhibited distinctive styles. The Dravidian style in the South, with its towering gopurams and elaborately carved temple complexes, contrasted

with the Rajput forts and palaces characterized by ornate frescoes and architectural embellishments. The regional architectural styles were a reflection of cultural, climatic, and historical influences unique to each area.

5) **Artistic Techniques and Materials:**
Artists across regions utilized a diverse range of materials and techniques. Bronze and stone were prevalent in South Indian sculptures, while the Rajput and Pahari schools excelled in miniature paintings. Each region had its expertise, such as the delicate metalwork of Kashmir and the terracotta artistry of Bengal, contributing to the diversity of medieval Indian art.

6) **Cultural Exchange and Influences:**
Trade routes facilitated cultural exchanges, resulting in the amalgamation of diverse artistic influences. The Mughal Empire, for instance, synthesized Persian and Indian aesthetics in its artwork, influencing regional styles. These exchanges led to artistic innovation and the emergence of hybrid styles in different regions.

7) **Artistic Themes and Subjects:**
Regional art often depicted themes intrinsic to the local culture and folklore. Pahari paintings portrayed tales from the hills, while Rajasthani art showcased courtly life, royal portraits, and religious narratives. These themes were intricately woven into the fabric of regional art, reflecting the societal ethos and values.

8) **Art as a Reflection of Socio-economic Life:**
Artistic expressions reflected the socio-economic life of the regions. Paintings, sculptures, and architectural marvels depicted agricultural practices, festivals, courtly scenes, and religious rituals, offering glimpses into the societal structures and everyday lives of the people.

9) **Artistic Innovation and Evolution:**
Regional art witnessed constant innovation and evolution. Schools of art developed, artists experimented with new techniques, and styles evolved over time. This evolution reflected the adaptability and dynamism of the artists, leading to the refinement and diversification of regional art forms.

10) **Legacy and Preservation:**
Efforts in contemporary times aim to preserve and promote the legacy of regional art. Museums, cultural institutions, and government initiatives work toward conserving artworks, documenting traditions, and educating people about the significance of these art forms, ensuring their preservation for posterity. These initiatives highlight the enduring legacy and cultural importance of medieval India's diverse regional artistry.

3.7.2 Regional Architecture:

Regional architecture is not only a representation of a place's physical structures but also a testament to its culture, heritage, and adaptation to the environment. Its preservation is crucial for maintaining cultural identities and passing down invaluable knowledge about sustainable design practices. The development of regional architecture in medieval India was marked by distinct styles, influenced by local cultures, traditions, available materials, and patronage from ruling dynasties. Here's an in-depth look at the evolution of regional architecture:

1) **Dravidian Architecture in South India:**
   Dravidian architecture, prominent in South India, showcased temple complexes with towering gopurams (entrance gateways), intricate carvings, and colossal halls. The temples, like the Brihadeshwara Temple in Thanjavur, emphasized grandeur, with pyramid-shaped vimanas (towers) and intricate sculptures portraying mythological narratives.

2) **Indo-Islamic Architecture in North India:**
   The advent of Indo-Islamic architecture introduced elements like domes, minarets, and arches. The Qutub Minar in Delhi, a UNESCO World Heritage Site, exemplifies this style with its towering minaret adorned with intricate calligraphy and Islamic motifs, reflecting the fusion of Indian and Islamic architectural traditions.

3) **Rajput Architecture in Rajasthan:**
   Rajput architecture focused on forts, palaces, and havelis characterized by ornate facades, frescoes, and intricate jharokhas (overhanging balconies). Examples include the Amber Fort in Jaipur, showcasing the fusion of Hindu and Mughal architectural elements, featuring ornate gates and opulent palaces.

4) **Mughal Architecture in North India:**
   Mughal architecture, epitomized by monuments like the Taj Mahal and Red Fort, blended Persian, Islamic, and Indian styles. It showcased symmetrical gardens, intricate marble inlay work, domes, and minarets. The harmonious fusion of materials and designs symbolized opulence and grandeur.

5) **Vijayanagara Architecture in Deccan:**
   The Vijayanagara Empire in the Deccan region left a legacy of grand temples and civic structures. Hampi, the capital, boasts awe-inspiring temple complexes like the Virupaksha Temple, featuring ornate pillars, monolithic structures, and detailed sculptures.

6) **Pallava and Chola Architecture in Tamil Nadu:**
   Tamil Nadu witnessed remarkable architectural contributions from the Pallavas and Cholas. The Shore Temple in Mahabalipuram, built by the Pallavas, showcases structural elegance, intricate carvings, and monolithic sculptures, while Chola temples like the Brihadeshwara Temple highlight exceptional temple planning and stone carvings.

7) **Bengal Sultanate Architecture:**
   Bengal Sultanate architecture reflected a fusion of indigenous Bengal styles with Islamic elements. The Sixty Dome Mosque (Shat Gombuj Masjid) in Bagerhat,

Bangladesh, exhibits a unique blend of domes, arches, and terracotta ornamentation, portraying the regional architectural heritage.

8) **Gujarat Architecture:**

The architectural heritage of Gujarat featured elements like stepwells (vavs), intricate stone carvings, and ornate Islamic-influenced structures. The Rani ki Vav in Patan, a UNESCO World Heritage Site, exemplifies Gujarati craftsmanship with its elaborate carvings and architectural grandeur.

9) **Pahari Architecture in the Himalayan Region:**

Pahari architecture in the Himalayan region emphasized wooden temples, wall paintings, and intricate carvings. The architectural style showcased in temples like the Raghunath Temple in Kullu and Naggar Castle reflected the artistic prowess of the Pahari artisans.

10) **Legacy and Preservation Efforts:**

Efforts in contemporary times focus on conserving and documenting regional architectural marvels. Preservation initiatives, restoration projects, and UNESCO recognitions highlight the importance of safeguarding these architectural treasures, ensuring their legacy for future generations. These architectural styles collectively represent the diverse and culturally rich tapestry of medieval Indian architecture.

♦♦♦

Review Questions

Q.1. Answer the Following Questions:

1) Explain in detail about the Qila-i-Kunha Masjid.
2) Discuss about the Tombs of Hasan Sur.
3) Explain the Tombs of Sher Shah.
4) Explain in detail about the Art and Architecture during Akbar.
5) Write about the Tomb of Humayan.
6) Discuss Features and Importance of Fort.
7) Explain in detail about the Fatehpur Sikri.
8) Discuss about the Allahabad Fort.
9) Explain in detail about the Lahore Fort.
10) Explain about the Art and Architecture during Jahangir.
11) Discuss about the Sikandara.
12) Explain in detail the Tomb of Itmad-ud-Daula.
13) Discuss about the Art and Architecture during Shahjahan.
14) Explain the Features and Importance of Taj Mahal.
15) Discuss about the Features and Importance of Red Fort.
16) Explain in detail about the Jama Masjid.
17) Write in detail about Mughal Painting.
18) Discuss about the Regional Art and & Architecture in Medieval India.

Q.2. Write Short Notes on:

1) Qila-ul-Kunha Masjid.
2) Tombs of Hasan Sur.
3) Tombs of Sher Shah.
4) Akbar.
5) Tomb of Hunayan.
6) Agra Fort.
7) Fatehpur Sikri.
8) Allahabad Fort.
9) Lahore Fort.
10) Jahangir.
11) Sikandara.
12) Tomb of Itmad-ud-Masjid.
13) Mughal Painting.
14) Regional Art & Architecture.

♦♦♦